20/20 Crafts & Object Talks

That Teach About God's Power

Susan L. Lingo

www.susanlingobooks.com

> We will tell the next generation the praiseworthy deeds of the Lord, his power, and the wonders he has done.
> —Psalm 78:4

20/20 Crafts & Object Talks That Teach About God's Power

© 2007 Susan L. Lingo

Published by Susan Lingo Books, Loveland, Colorado 80538.
All rights reserved. No part of this book may be reproduced in any manner without written permission from the publisher, except where noted in the text and in the case of brief quotations embodied in critical articles and reviews.

Interior design and cover by Susan L. Lingo

All Scripture quotations, unless otherwise noted, are taken from the HOLY BIBLE, NEW INTERNATIONAL VERSION®, NIV®. Copyright © 1973, 1978, 1984 by International Bible Society. Used by permission of Zondervan Publishing House. All rights reserved.

16 15 14 13 12 11 10 09 08 07   5 4 3 2 1
ISBN 978-0-9760696-3-8
Printed in the United States of America

Contents

CRAFTS 6

House On the Rock (Matthew 7:24) 8

On-the-Mend Kits (Psalm 34:18; Jeremiah 30:17) 10

Trinity Power Bracelet (Psalms 54:4, 118:7; Matthew 28:19, 20) 12

You're-Surrounded Snuggler (Psalms 32:10, 125:2) 14

Love Bears All Things (Psalm 36:5; 1 Corinthians 13:4-7) 16

Personalized Fan Pulls (John 10:3) 18

Covered Candles (Psalms 91, 116:6) 20

Sweet & Sour Frames (Matthew 5:43-48) 22

Key to Resisting (1 Peter 3:11; James 4:7) 24

Good Fruit Apples (Luke 8:15; Galatians 5:22, 23) 26

Sure Signs of God's Power (Psalms 25:4, 43:3) 28

Sudz-n-Dudz (Ezekiel 36:29; 2 Timothy 2:20, 21) 30

The Prayer Trellis (Exodus 22:27; Psalm 10:17) 32

Lovin' Those Details! (Matthew 6:25-34) 34

Fitting-Plans Serving Bowl (Proverbs 23:18; Jeremiah 29:11) 36

Rock-Solid Forgiveness (Psalm 18:2; Matthew 6:14, 15; Romans 4:7) 38

Prayer Pockets (Proverbs 3:5; Jeremiah 33:3) 40

The Ring of Victory (Philippians 2:10, 11; 1 Corinthians 15:57) 42

No Eggheads Here! (Proverbs 2:6, 3:13, 8:11) 44

3-in-1 to Overcome! (Job 12:13; Colossians 1:13, 14; Romans 15:13) 46

OBJECT TALKS 48

Here and Back Prayers (Psalms 34:4, 118:21; Jeremiah 33:3) 50

Resist 'n Run! (1 Peter 3:11; James 4:7, 8) 52

Superbly Surrounded (Psalm 32:10, 125:2) 54

The Sweetest Teacher (Psalm 119:103; 2 Timothy 3:16, 17) 56

Multiply His Love! (Romans 12:10, 13:8; Ephesians 4:32) 58

Forever Forgiven (Psalm 103:12; Romans 4:7; Colossians 1:13, 14) 60

Jesus Frees Us! (Romans 6:18, 22, 8:2) 62

Help = Love (Galatians 5:13; 1 Thessalonians 5:14; Hebrews 6:10) 64

The Victory Is the Lord's! (Psalm 24:8; Ephesians 6:13-18) 66

The Road to Guidance (Psalms 25:5, 43:3) 68

Rising to Heaven (Psalm 141:2) 70

Any Way, We're Okay! (Matthew 5:43-48) 72

Healed Hearts (Psalm 34:18; Jeremiah 30:17) 74

Perfect Planning (Proverbs 23:18; Jeremiah 29:11) 76

Not-So-Fishy Names (John 10:3) 78

The Clean Machine (2 Timothy 2:20, 21) 80

Guardian Angels (Psalm 91:9-16) 82

Stop the Pop! (Matthew 6:25-34) 84

Wisecream Cones (Proverbs 2:6. 3:13, 8:11) 86

Choice Obedience (Psalm 119:57, 66) 88

Index of Themes & Activities 90

SECTION 1: CRAFTS

Crafts make awesome teaching tools—and are more than memorable for kids!

Aligning cool crafts with biblical themes and memorable messages gives kids double the learning fun. And it's so easy to do, too! Simply focus on a biblical theme or choose one you're working on in class, then match up a craft from the many to choose from this unique resource, and you're on the way to turning ordinary craft time into powerful teaching time—with concrete reminders kids carry home to their families.

These crafts won't sit still!

Each craft project included in *20/20 Crafts & Object Talks That Teach About God's Power* offers solid, Bible-based learning in the form of cool crafts kids enjoy making. Age-appropriate, skill-appropriate, and loaded with creative fun, these are craft projects that won't sit still! Many of these crafts can be used as serving projects, some are used to play games, and others can be given as gifts. Each craft is based on an attribute of God's power to help kids know, love, and obey God more closely while building their faith in God's perfect plans and power. Use these crafts to enrich a Bible lesson you're learning, reinforce what kids are discovering about God's power, or as accompaniments to specific Scripture verses. You'll find a handy *Activities and Themes Index* at the back of the book to help you match up crafts and themes—and the *Contents* page lists the various Scripture verses used in each craft project.

Kids long to discover the true nature of God—and these cool crafts will help make the learning memorable!

Have fun teaching your kids about God's perfect power through creative crafts—and watch the smiles *and* your kids' faith grow!

House On the Rock
Matthew 7:24

God's Power... Helps us obey Him

Simple Supplies

- baby food jars with lids
- rocks or smooth stones (one to fit inside each jar)
- tiny plastic houses, thimbles or plastic blocks (to make tiny houses from)
- fine-tipped, permanent markers
- water
- florist's clay
- glitter
- craft glue & scissors
- copies of the verse card on the opposite page

MAKING THE CRAFT

Collect the craft materials. Photocopy the verse card on the facing page one per craft project. As you collect rocks or stones, choose ones that are flat on opposite ends or sides. You may wish to make one of these nifty house-in-a-jar projects to show to kids as you explain the craft directions.

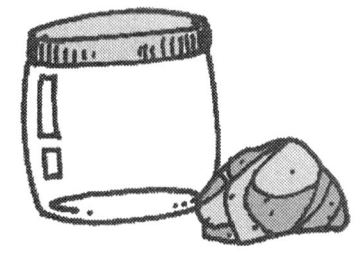

For each project, place a small wad of florist's clay on the bottom edge of a rock or stone and push it inside the bottom of a clean, empty jar. Use another small wad of florist's clay to attach a tiny house on top of the stone. (If you are making tiny houses from small plastic blocks or thimbles, add windows and doors to the houses using fine-tipped permanent markers. See the *20/20 Tip on the next page* for more suggestions for the tiny houses.)

Fill the jar half full with water and sprinkle a bit of glitter in the water if desired. Run a bead of glue around the inside edge of the lid then twist the lid securely on the jar.

Finally, cut out the verse card and fold as indicated. Glue the flaps of the card to the jar lid so the card stands upright and the verse can be read from the front of the jar. Let the jar dry completely, then shake it to see how the house stands firm even when swirling waters surround it!

MAKING THE POINT

As the craft projects dry, invite volunteers to read aloud the parable of the Wise and Foolish Builders from Matthew 7: 24-28. Challenge kid to give a brief description of what the parable teaches us and why those lessons are important. Then ask:

- In what ways did the wise builder use obedience to build his house?
- How did being obedient and wise help the man who built his house on rock?
- In what ways does being obedient to God's Word help us stay away from troubles, temptations, evil, and sin?
- What are ways we can be obedient to God and His Word?

When the jars are dry, shake them gently as you repeat the following rhyme about being wise and obedient:

The man who built his house on rock
Was saved on that rainy day—
To stay out of harm when we build our lives,
We must turn to God and obey!

Fold outward

Fold back

Everyone who hears these things I say and obeys them is like a wise man who built his house on rock.

—Matthew 7:24-38

Fold outward

Use tiny houses from old games or make your own using dice cubes, hair spray caps, or even square pencil erasers! Add details with permanent markers, paints, or sequins. Use hot glue guns to help odd-shaped houses sit solidly on the rocks or stones.

On-the-Mend Kits

Psalm 34:18, 147:3; Jeremiah 30:17

God's Power...

Heals us in many ways

Simple Supplies

- medium sized sliding matchboxes
- small buttons
- squares of craft felt
- large sequins or confetti
- scissors
- safety pins
- sewing needles
- colored threads
- poster board or cardboard
- tacky craft glue
- fine-tipped markers
- copies of the verse cards on opposite page (optional)

MAKING THE CRAFT

These great little sewing kits are as much fun to make as they are useful! Use this craft to help kids understand that only God has the power to heal us and mend broken hearts and spirits.

To prepare and assemble each miniature sewing kit, cut a long strip of craft felt the same width as the matchbox. Wrap the outside of the matchbox with the felt, overlapping the ends a half inch. Cut the strip to remove the excess felt. Cover the matchbox in sticky craft glue, then wrap the felt around the box making sure the ends overlap on the bottom of the box. (Do not cover the ends where the box slides in and out of the matchbox cover.)

Glue two or three small buttons and several sequins or large confetti bits to the top of the matchbox as decorations. Carefully slide the "drawer" out from the matchbox, then set the felt-covered frame aside to dry for several minutes.

Place the drawer on a piece of poster board or cardboard and trace around the base. Cut out the rectangle, cutting it a bit smaller than the base of the drawer. Wrap colored thread around the poster board or cardboard rectangle. Use several colors of thread including white and black. Place the thread-wrapped rectangle in the bottom of the matchbox drawer.

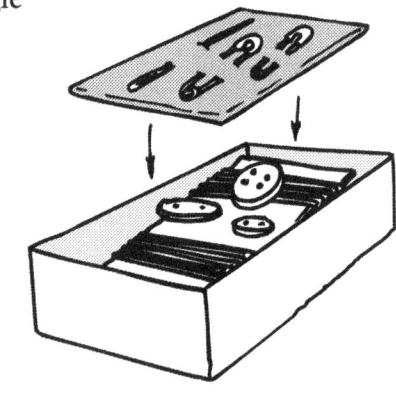

Cut a 1-inch felt square to fit inside the box and poke two needles through the felt. Pin a couple of safety pins to the piece of felt. Use various sizes of safety pins if possible. Place the felt square, needles, and pins in the matchbox drawer on top of the thread card.

Choose several small buttons to place in the sewing kit. Including a variety of colored buttons will assure different shirts, jackets, and blouses may be mended—and matched!

When the matchbox cover is dry, carefully slide the drawer containing the sewing items into the matchbox cover. If desired, copy, color, and cut out the verse card below to include with each kit. Now, isn't this craft "sew" clever and useful?

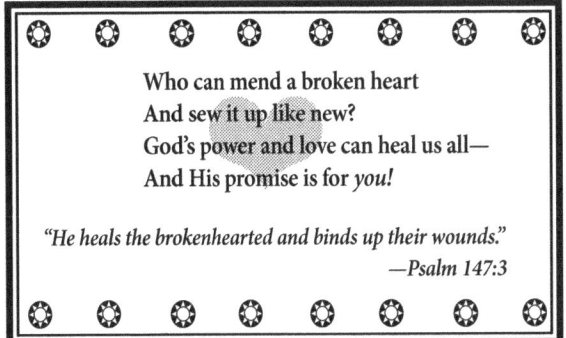

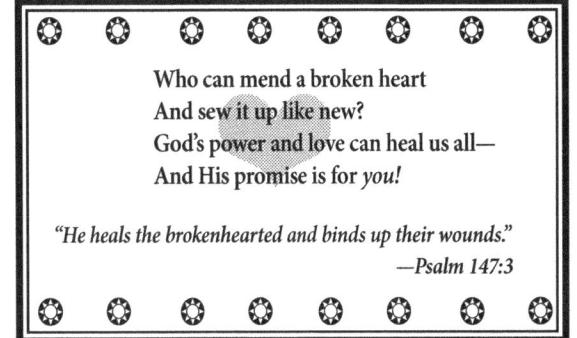

MAKING THE POINT

Hold up a sheet of paper and a piece of craft felt. Ask kids which is easier to fix or mend if it's torn: a sheet of paper or a piece of fabric. Encourage kids to tell why they feel as they do. Then ask:

✂ **What can mend or fix feelings when they're hurt?**

✂ **What can mend a broken heart or a hurt spirit?**

✂ **In what ways can only God truly mend a broken heart, a hurt spirit, or our feelings?**

Explain that once a paper or fabric is torn, even mending it with tape or a needle and thread can leave marks or scars. Point out that only God has the power to heal us completely so that we have no scars and we become better than new! Tell kids that when we have whole, healed, healthy hearts, spirits, and lives, we can serve God more completely and joyously.

Invite volunteers to read aloud Psalms 34:18 and 147:3, and Jeremiah 30:17. Then briefly discuss ways God heals us and ways we can show God our thankfulness for His gift of healing. Challenge kids to remember, each time they use their sewing kits, that only God has the power to heall and mend us in every way.

Consider making this craft as a cool service project and present your kits to missionaries or others who would be "sew" happy to receive them!

These tiny sewing kits are ideal to present to traveling missionaries or others who visit your church. Add a card that says: *We "sew" appreciate all you do for God's Kingdom!* Consider making these handy kits for military men and women who are serving God and their country abroad.

Trinity Power Bracelet
Psalm 54:4, 118:7; Matthew 28:19, 20

God's Power...

Helps us day and night

Simple Supplies

- boxes of thin, small paper clips (approximately 20-30 clips per child)
- packages of tiny seed beads in red, purple, blue, black and yellow (at least two packages of each color)
- muffin tins
- small heart charms
- small metal washers
- twist-tie wires
- scissors

MAKING THE CRAFT

Collect several boxes of small paper clips and tiny seed-beads in a variety of colors. Place the seed-beads and paper clips in muffin tins so several kids can choose colors at the same time and to keep the beads from spilling. You may wish to make a Trinity Bracelet of your own to show as a sample.

Before beginning the craft project, hold up a red, blue, and purple bead (or point to the ones on your sample bracelet). Ask kids what color bead might be good to symbolize God, Jesus, and the Holy Spirit. Encourage kids to explain their choices. Then tell kids that God's power is expressed through the Trinity: through God Himself, through His Son Jesus, and through His Spirit. Explain that red is a vibrant, powerful color and red beads will be used to symbolize God. Point to the purple bead and explain that Jesus' royalty as God's Son is symbolized by the color purple. Finally, tell kids that, like air, we can't see the Holy Spirit with our eyes, but we *can* see His power to help us by what the Spirit accomplishes through us and others. Explain that blue beads will symbolize the helping power of the Holy Spirit. Show kids the black and yellow beads and explain that these colors represent day and night—which is when God's power is there to help us!

To make each Trinity Power Bracelet, have kids thread one of each color bead onto paper clips (red, purple, blue, yellow, and black). Each paper clip should have all five colors.

Direct kids to prepare twenty paper clips to begin with, then link the clips together. Try the bracelet on around your wrist to see if it will fit. Add more beaded paper clips as needed so the bracelet is long enough to slip over your wrist.

When the bracelet fits around your wrist, link the end paper clips together. Use twist-tie wires to add charms to the Trinity Power Bracelets. (If you can't find heart charms or small washers, copy the patterns below to use instead.) Have girls use heart-shaped charms to symbolize the loving help God sends. Let boys use small metal washer "charms" to represent the never-ending (like a circle) help God promises us when we trust in His power. Snip off excess wire. Finally, slide the bracelets on over your hands.

MAKING THE POINT

Read aloud Psalm 54:4 and 118:7, and John 14:16, Matthew 28:19, 20. Ask kids to explain how God, Jesus, and the Holy Spirit each help us through their ultimate and perfect power. Then ask:

- How does God's power help us be faithful and obedient?
- In what ways do Jesus' power to love and forgive help us?
- How does the power of the Holy Spirit help us serve God and others?

Remind kids that God's power to help us is perfect. Brainstorm ways God helps us in difficult times as well as in our day-to-day lives. Encourage kids to tell about times God's power helped them and how it felt to know that God, Jesus, and the Holy Spirit were there for them. Remind kids that God expresses His power through the Trinity—and that no team could even offer the help and hope we find in God, Jesus, and the Holy Spirit! And the best part? Our divine Power Team is ready to help us day or night forever!

Encourage kids to wear their color-coded bracelets as reminders of God's power to help us day and night.

TRY THIS IDEA!

Color-coding beads, buttons, and more on craft projects helps kids remember the point you're trying to make—and the colors are bright and inviting. Invite kids to make their own beaded bracelets or rings and assign colors and meanings to their projects. Be sure to let kids share and show their projects as the tell about the significance of the colors!

You're-Surrounded Snuggler
Psalms 32:10, 125:2

God's Power... Surrounds us

Simple Supplies

- men's neckties (one per craft)
- scissors & tacky craft glue
- self-adhesive hook & loop fastener dots
- plastic sunglasses (optional)
- glitter glue (optional)

MAKING THE CRAFT

For this unique craft project, collect old, wide neckties. Visit used clothing stores or ask members of the congregation to donate their wide, out-of-style neckties. You'll need one necktie for each craft project. You may wish to make a glasses snuggler before class as a sample. Kids may enjoy working in pairs as they make these cool eyeglasses or sunglasses snugglers.

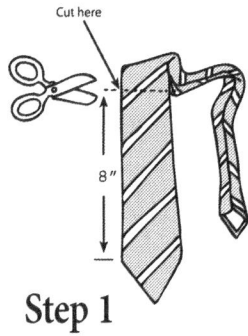

Step 1

For each snuggler, cut a 12-inch long section from the wider end of a necktie, measuring from the pointed tip upward (Step 1).

If the tie has a tag inside, remove it using scissors. If the seam is unraveling a bit, seal it with tacky glue.

Step 2

Next, glue the straight opening of the tie closed using tacky craft glue (Step 2). You may need to hold the edges together for a few minutes until the glue dries. This will make the bottom of the glasses snuggler so be sure the opening is completely sealed or your glasses may slip out!

Step 3

Press two sticky-backed hook and loop fastener dots to the wide end of the tie—one on the inside portion of the tip and one on the seam of the tie (Step 3). These will keep the cases closed and the glasses safe inside!

Show kids how to slide a pair of eyeglasses or sunglasses into the snuggler, then fold down the flap and press on the hook and loop dots to fasten the case closed.

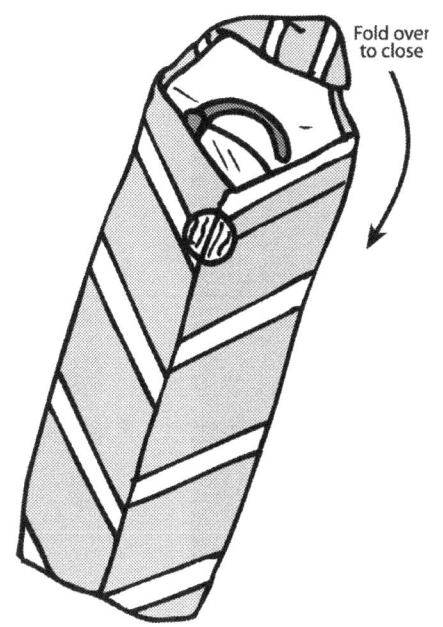

MAKING THE POINT

Invite a volunteer to stand in the center of the room, then have everyone stand around that person. Ask kids what it means to be surrounded, like the person in the center of the group. Encourage kids to tell how being surrounded by love, support, and kindness would feel. Point out that if we're surrounded by love it means that nothing bad can truly hurt us and we're never really alone. Have everyone sit down except the volunteer. Ask that person how standing alone feels and how it differs from being surrounded by friends. Then have the volunteer sit down with the group. Ask:

- In what ways does God and His power surround us each day?
- How does knowing that God's love, power, forgiveness, and mercy surrounds you help strengthen your faith?
- In what ways would not having God's surrounding love change the way you live or your spirit of hope? Explain.
- How can knowing that God surrounds us help today with a problem or special challenge you might be facing?

Remind kids that just as a glasses case surrounds the glasses and covers them with protection, so God's power and love surround and cover us. Read aloud Psalm 32:10 and 125:2. Challenge kids to keep their eyeglasses or sunglasses in the protective snugglers to surround them and keep them from harm. Offer a prayer thanking God for His surrounding power and love.

TRY THIS! Let kids embellish inexpensive sunglasses to keep inside their snugglers. Use glitter glue to decorate the glasses and add sparkle to the snugglers, too!

Love Bears All Things
Psalm 36:5; 1 Corinthians 13:4-7

MAKING THE CRAFT

Before making this craft, photocopy the verse cards on the opposite page on stiff cardstock or construction paper. Draw a couple of large heart shapes on poster board (at least 10-inches across), then cut out the shapes. These are patterns kids will use to trace and cut their own poster board hearts from. Purchase a couple of bags of gummi candy bears or a couple of boxes of small, teddy-shaped cookies. Each project requires about 6-10 candies or cookies.

Have kids use the poster board heart patterns to trace and cut out a pair of matching hearts. Place on heart on top of the other matching the outlines, then tape the hearts together at a few places around the edge. (This will hold the hearts together as kids work to punch holes and "sew" the hearts together.)

Using markers, direct kids to make tiny dots along the side a bottom edges of the hearts (do not include the heats "humps" at the top edge). Make the dots about a half an inch apart. Punch a hole for each dot around the heart. Then cut a 2-foot length of yarn for each project and tie a large knot in one end of each length. Lace the unknotted ends through the holes in the hearts, lacing the edges together. When you've laced through the last hole, tie or slide the end of the yarn under the laces and snip off excess yarn.

God's Power...

Simple Supplies

- pink, white, or red poster board
- scissors
- clear tape
- hole punch
- markers
- colored yarn
- sandwich bags
- gummi bears or teddy-shaped cookies
- copies of the verse card on the opposite page
- curling ribbon (optional)

Decorate the hearts using markers, then write "Love 'bears' all!" on one side and "1 Corinthians 13:4-7" on the other. Then have each person place several gummi bears or bear-shaped cookies in sandwich bags. (Tie the ends of the sandwich bags with colorful curling ribbon if desired). Slide the treats into the open tops of the hearts. Then color a verse card to slip in each paper heart.

Try This Idea!

These adorable crafts make sweet Valentine reminders of God's love for us—and out love for Him. Use them as gifts for parents, church leaders, or adults who volunteer in your classroom.

MAKING THE POINT

Challenge kids to brainstorm a list of what qualities the perfect love should have. Suggestions might include patience, hope, happiness, giving, and forgiveness. Then ask if it's possible for people to love others in perfect ways. Encourage kids to explain their thoughts. Then explain that we love because God loved us first. Point out that only God has the power to love us perfectly and in every way. Ask:

- ✂ Why do you think God is able to love us so perfectly?
- ✂ How can God's all-accepting, all-forgiving love change our lives?
- ✂ In what ways does God teach us to love others through His powerful love for us?

Invite volunteers to read aloud 1 Corinthians 13:4-7 and Psalm 36:5. Briefly describe the kind of love God desires us to have and how His own love for us is even bigger. Remind kids that God's powerful love has the power to forgive us and bear with us even when we don't always make good choices or have sinned. Remind kids that God's greatest demonstration of His powerful, forgiving love was His gift of Jesus and the offer of eternal life! As kids enjoy their treats, name ways that God's perfect love bears with us even when we're not perfect.

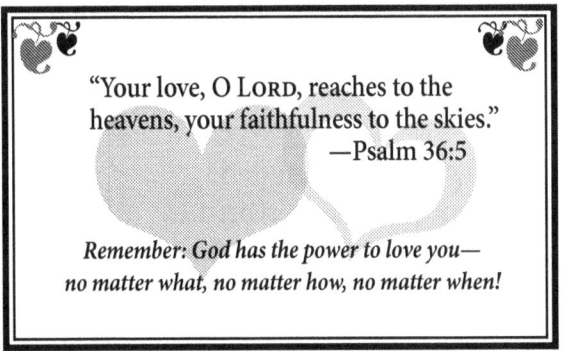

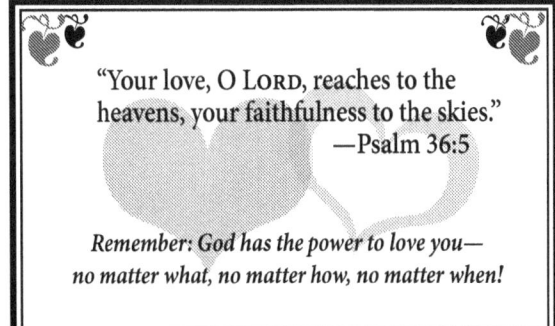

Personalized Fan Pulls
John 10:3

God's Power... Calls us by name

Simple Supplies

- plastic or satin ornament balls (1 or 2 per person)
- permanent markers
- glitter glue pens
- paint pens
- paper or foam egg cartons
- scissors
- colored ribbon
- yarn, wire, or small chain (2-feet per project)
- twist-tie wires
- newspapers

MAKING THE CRAFT

Before class, be sure you have a 2-foot length of yarn, wire, or small chain for each person. These will be used as hangers for the fan pulls. (You may need to explain to kids that fan or light pulls hook onto ceiling switches to turn on a ceiling fan or light fixture.) You'll also need to have a colorful selection of ribbon. Girls may enjoy using curling ribbon and boys may prefer straight ribbon which will look like fringe on the crafts. Provide several colors of ribbon. Cover tables with newspapers. Cut apart the paper or foam egg cartons so each person has an egg cup.

Set out the markers, paint pens, and glitter glue pens. Hand each person an ornament ball and egg cup. Explain to kids that they'll be decorating ornament balls using the craft items, then writing their names on one side of the balls and John 10:3 on the other side. Simple designs such as stars, swirls, hearts, flowers, dots, and stripes work well when decorating the ornament balls.

When the ornaments are decorated (and before names are added), place the balls in the egg carton cup to dry for several minutes, or kids can hold the balls and blow on them to speed drying time.

When the ornaments are dry, have kids write their names on one side of the balls using permanent marker or paint pens, then write "John 10:3" on the other side. (After the paint dries, kids may wish to outline the names using glitter glue pens.)

Cut various lengths and colors of ribbon. Tie them together at one end, then use a twist-tie wire to attach the ribbons to the top loops on the ornaments.

Finally, add a 2-foot length of yarn, wire, or small chain to the top loops of the ornaments by securing them with twist-tie wires. Tell kids they can tie the loose end of the yarn or wire to the pull on a ceiling fan (have adults help with this). If you used chain, tell kids to attach the ends to the fan or light pulls using twist-tie wires. If kids would rather, they can hang their special name pulls on a curtain rod or in a window.

MAKING THE POINT

If you have an extra ornamet ball, have kids stand in a circle and toss the ball to one another across the circle calling out the person's name you're tossing to. (Use a paper wad or eraser if you don't have a ball.) After everyone has caught and tossed the ball at least one time, Aask kids if they know what their names mean. Allow everyone to share, then explain that there are many different, unique, and even unusual names in the world. Ask if they think anyone could possibly know everyone's name. Then tell kids that God has the power to know each person's name, what dreams and hopes lie in their hearts, and their every thought! Then ask:

✂ **How does it feel to know God knows your name and everything about you?**

✂ **What do you think it means when the Bible tells us that God "calls us by name"?**

Read aloud John 10:3, then offer a prayer thanking God for knowing you so well. Challenge kids to hang up their craft projects at home and each time they see it to remember that God knows and calls them by name.

TRY THIS! Kids may enjoy making another simple, personalized picture to hang up. Simply let kids paint a background design on wood or canvas, then write their names in black marker or paint. Add glitter and ribbons, then hang on a wall or door.

Covered Candles

Psalms 91, 116:6

God's Power... Protects us

Simple Supplies

- large aluminum pie pans (one per person)
- small aluminum pie pans or glass saucers (one per person)
- small and medium sized nails
- tea light candles (one per person)
- matches (for adult use only)

MAKING THE CRAFT

Place craft items on a sturdy table or plan to work on the floor. Be sure you have flexible, aluminum pie pans for kids to use and not thick tins. Kids will be poking nails through the aluminum pans, so the disposable aluminum pie pans work best for this craft project. You'll need one large pan and a smaller one for each person. (Make sure the larger pans will cover the smaller pans or the small saucers if you choose to use them.) You may wish to make one of these candle projects before class and light it so kids can see how the light shines through the holes. Turn out the lights to make the room as dark as possible before lighting the candle. Leave the candle lit, if possible, during the *Making the Point* section.

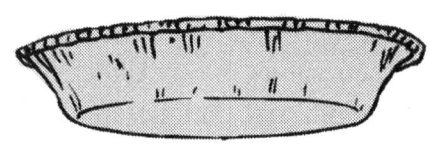

Hand each person a large and small pie pan and a nail. Direct kids to turn the larger pie pans upside down on the table or floor. Show kids how to gently poke the nails through the sides and tops (actually the bottoms of the pie pans) to make designs. Caution kids to keep their designs simple. Heart shapes, stars, or dotty designs work best.

When the designs are completed, hand each person a small, tea light candle to place in the small aluminum pie pan or on a glass saucer. Explain that when the candle is lit and the larger pan covers the candle, the light will shine through the nail holes

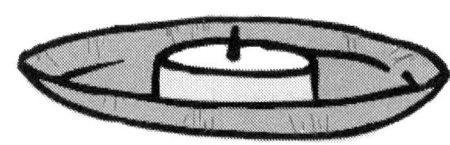

in beautiful patterns! Tell kids to have their parents light the candles at home for a lovely dinner time centerpiece.

MAKING THE POINT

Gather kids in a circle and place the candle in the center of the circle on the floor. (Be sure the small aluminum pie pan or saucer is under the candle.) Light the candle, then invite kids to blow and see if they can put out the flame. Point out that if a flame isn't protected from the wind, it will be blown out and cannot be used to light our way. Relight the candle, then ask what can be done to protect the flame from being blown out. Suggestions might include placing it in a glass with tall sides, in a lantern, or under the pie plate with the holes. Carefully place the large aluminum pie pan over the tea light candle. Then ask:

- ✂ **How is the pie pan protecting the candle's flame?**
- ✂ **In what ways does God protect us by covering us with His power and protection?**
- ✂ **Is anything we face or any problem we run into bigger than God's power to protect us? Explain.**
- ✂ **How does having God's protection around us help us be more brave in our faith?**

TRY THIS IDEA!

If you have younger children and wish to steer clear of using candles even at home, simply turn this cool craft into a window hanger by poking a hole at the center top edge of each larger pie pan. (You can omit both the candle and the smaller pan or plate.) Thread a 10-inch length of yearn or cord through the hole and tie the ends into a hanging loop. The sunlight will shine through the holes nicely!

Invite a volunteer to read aloud Psalm 116:6. Then tell kids that Psalm 91 praises God for the power of His protection and how He saves us. Invite several volunteers to read Psalm 91, or have the whole class read this beautiful psalm of protection in unison.

Challenge kids to place their Covered Candles on a table at home (the dining table if possible) and have their parents light the candles as the family sits to share a meal. Tell kids to invite family members to name ways that God protects us or to share how God has saved them from temptations, troubles, and other difficult times or situations in their lives.

Sweet & Sour Frames
Matthew 5:43-48

God's Power...  Accepts us

Simple Supplies

- 5-by-7-inch plastic picture frames
- tacky craft glue
- white card stock paper (cut into 5-by-7-inch rectangles)
- permanent markers
- water-based markers
- crayons
- pencils
- bags of colorful sweet candies and sour candies

MAKING THE CRAFT

Before class, be sure you have an inexpensive plastic picture frame each person. These can be found most craft or discount stores. You may also use thick poster board or foam board cut into 5-by-7-inch frames. Be sure there are hangers at the backs of the frames. (Poster or foam board frames may be stuck to a wall using sticky tack or simply leaned upright against a book.) You'll also need a colorful variety of flat, hard sweet and sour (both kinds) candies such as ones with swirls, flowers, or stripes. Candy discs and hearts work especially well, although ribbon and cut-rock candies add a nice touch!

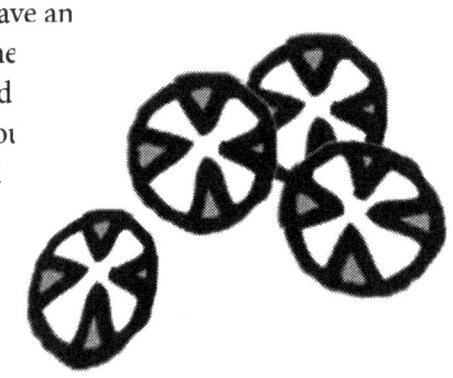

Hand each person a picture frame. Direct kids to color the frames using permanent markers if desired. Then glue candies around the edges of the frames. As kids work to add color and candies to their frames, challenge them to chat about people in their lives who are sweet and inviting, like sweet pieces of candy.

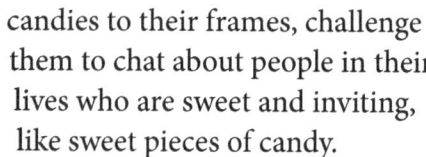

When the frames are completed, distribute 5-by-7-inch pieces of white card stock. Invite kids to draw, on one side of their papers, a picture of someone in their lives who they think is sweet or who treats them sweetly. Then flip the papers over and have each person draw a picture of someone who may be harder to love or who may be "sour". These people may be someone at school who acts in bully-ish ways or someone who isn't friendly, doesn't share, or has a hurtful spirit. Remind kids that caring for others who aren't as sweet as candy can be tough, but that everyone needs love—both sweet and sour alike. When the pictures are completed, form a circle while the frames continue drying. (You'll place the pictures in the frames later.)

MAKING THE POINT

Have everyone hold up the pictures of the people who treat them in sweet ways. Briefly discuss what makes a person act sweetly or what qualities draw them near others in positive ways. Then flip the pictures over and discuss possible reasons some people act in sour ways. (Don't mention the names of any people in the pictures.) Then ask:

- Why is it easier to like, be with, and even pray for the sweet people in our lives than the "unsweet" or sour ones?
- Why do you think God wants us to be kind to and to pray for our enemies and those who treat us in unkind ways?
- How can we treat others nicely who treat us in mean ways?
- What can you do this week to show the "unsweet" person in your picture that you care?
- What can you do this week to tell the sweet person in your picture that you care?

Older kids may enjoy making a "sweet & sour" class collage of people in the news or world who are both good and not-so-good. Explain the concept of *intercessory prayer* and how God calls us to pray for others—even the ones who are hard to pray for. Cut out pictures form magazines or newspapers or list their names, then pray for these people as a class.

Remind kids that of course it's easier to pray for, be kind to, and care about the people who are easy to love, but that God desires us to be kind, compassionate, and to pray for those people who are hard to love—or even to like! Place the pictures in the frames with the "unsweet" pictures showing. Then challenge kids to pray for the people in their pictures who are hard to love this week. Then flip the pictures over and pray for those who are easy to love the next week. Continue flipping and praying for those people for the next few weeks. Point out that our prayers, smiles, and encouragement may not change someone's actions, but they change our attitudes about "sour" people in *sweet* ways!

Key to Resisting
1 Peter 3:11; James 4:7

God's Power...

Helps us resist evil

Simple Supplies

- gray, self-hardening clay
- a plastic milk jug
- scissors
- small screws
- small screwdriver
- blank keys (one per person)
- fine-tipped permanent markers or fine-tipped paint pens
- plastic knives (optional)
- spray shellac (optional)

MAKING THE CRAFT

This unique and useful craft project will take two craft times as the clay must harden completely before adding the final touches. It may take a bit longer than some crafts—but is really worth it! Before class, be sure you have a golf-ball sized lump of self-hardening clay for each person. You'll also need a blank house or car key for each person. (If you choose not to use real keys, use the pattern on the opposite page.) You may wish to cut the flaps for the bottoms of the Keystones before class. For each flap, cut a 1.5-by-2.5-inch rectangle of plastic from an empty milk jug.

CRAFT TIME #1: Hand each person a lump of self-hardening clay. Direct kids to form the clay into a medium-sized "stone." Tell kids to smooth the surface of the stones and to make one side flat by pressing the clay stone gently on a table.

Show kids how to flip the stone over in their palms so the flat side is facing up. Gently push your finger into the bottom of the stone and dig away a small rectangle. Explain that this is the hiding place for a special key they will receive in a moment. Use the plastic knives to help carve a space large enough for a key (about 1.5-by-2.5-inches). Set aside the stone to dry until next class.

CRAFT TIME #2: Hand each person a key and a plastic flap. Help kids attach the flap to the bottom of the dried keystone using a small screw. (When the flap is swiveled, it will open and close, holding the key inside.) If you desire, use spray shellac to coat the keystones so they can be placed outside. (Spray the stones outdoors for ventilation!) Have kids use the fine-tipped markers or paint pens to write "James 4:7" on one side of the keys and 1 Peter 3:11 on the other. Blow on the keys to speed the drying time. When the keys are placed in the groove on the bottom of the keystones and the flap swiveled over them, they should stay safe and secure—and hidden! Tell kids they can use their keystones as paper weights on a desk to remind them that God gives us the key to resisting temptation and evil: *His power!* (If the stones have been coated with shellac, they can be placed in a garden or by a door and hold a spare door key.)

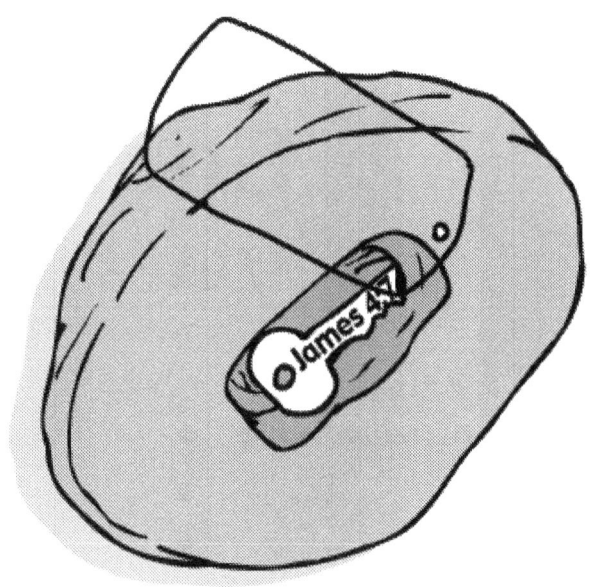

MAKING THE POINT

Ask kids what qualities or good things God desires us to have in our lives. Answers might include honesty, patience, compassion, faith, and obedience to God. Then ask kids what things God tells us to steer clear of or resist. Suggestions might include lies, cheating, swearing, mean thoughts and words, or disobedience to God. Ask:

- Is it always easy to resist the things God tells us are wrong? Explain.
- Why do you think God desires us to resist evil, temptation, and other negative things?
- How has God provided for us when it comes to resisting evil or steering clear of temptation?

Explain that God never leaves us without a plan and a purpose—and the power through Him! Remind kids that since God desires us to resist evil and temptation, He has provided us the key and that key is found in God's Word! Invite volunteers to read aloud 1 Peter 3:11 and James 4:7. Then discuss how drawing near to God and His power provide us the keys to turning from evil, temptation, and harm. Tell kids to remember these all-important keys each time they see their special keystones.

Use this key shape as a pattern if you choose not to use real keys. Photocopy the pattern onto stiff card stock, then carefully cut out the shape.

Good Fruit Apples
Luke 8:15; Galatians 5:22, 23

Simple Supplies

- scissors
- construction paper in red and white
- fishing line
- tape
- markers
- crayons
- photocopies of the apple and leaf pattern on the opposite page

MAKING THE CRAFT

Before class, photocopy the apple and leaf patterns from the opposite page. Use white and red construction paper for older kids, then let older kids cut green construction paper leaves. Younger kids can simply color the tops and bottoms of the apples red and the leaf pattern green using markers or crayons. Cut a 2-foot length of fishing line for each person.

Cut the apple pattern apart so you have a top and bottom section, plus three center sections and a leaf. Connect the pieces by taping them to fishing line. (Be sure the verse reads correctly down the apple.) Tape the leaf to the top portion of the apple (see illustration).

Suspend the apples from a window, ceiling fan, or doorway frame by taping the end of the fishing line in place.

MAKING THE POINT

Read Luke 8:15, then discuss the kinds of things God teaches us such as truth, faith, patience, compassion, and forgiveness. Ask kids why God is our greatest teacher and how we can be the best students ever. Ask:

- How do God's teachings affect our faith?
- Do you think God's teachings are always correct and relevant to our lives? Explain.

Invite volunteers to read aloud Galatians 5:22, 23. Then briefly discuss each good fruit and why it is a quality God desires us to have. Flip the apple mobiles over and write the list of good fruit of the Spirit on the backs of the apple sections. Challenge kids to name ways they can grow good fruit in their lives during the coming week. Tell kids to hang their Good Fruit Apple mobiles up at home to remind everyone in their families that God teaches us to grow, produce, and share good fruit with Him and with others.

TRY THIS IDEA!

Make other fruit pieces to add to your apple mobile. Oranges, lemons, grapes, strawberries, and bananas work well. On these fruit shapes, write verses that teach about different fruits of the Spirit. For example, write "Patience" at the top of a paper fruit. Then write the words to Proverbs 19:11 on the sections of that fruit.

Luke 8:15

"Those who hear God's teaching with a good, honest heart, obey God's teaching and patiently produce good fruit."

Permission to photocopy for church, school, or home use only. Taken from *20/20 Crafts and Object Talks That Teach About God's Power* © Susan Lingo, Susan Lingo Books, 2007.

Sure Signs of God's Power!

Psalms 25:5, 43:3

God's Power...

Directs & guides us

Simple Supplies

- poster board
- tape
- scissors & markers
- ¼-by-24-inch dowel rods (one per person)
- large disposable cups (one per person)
- glitter glue
- Plaster of Paris
- an old bucket & water
- a large spoon (to mix plaster)
- patterns for street signs (based on shapes from the opposite page)
- copies of the verse strips (from the opposite page)

MAKING THE CRAFT

Before class, be sure you have a large disposable cup for each person. (Large plastic cups used for picnics work well.) You'll need a 2-foot dowel rod for each person. (Shorter lengths can be used but will not be as impressive as they won't stick up tall as street signs usually do.) Enlarge the traffic signs on the opposite page onto poster board to use as patterns kids will trace on their own poster board. Photocopy the verse strips on the opposite page. Make several copies so kids can choose the verse they like best.

If you wish to omit the plaster, use cups filled with modeling dough or clay.

Just before craft time, mix a bucket of plaster of Paris according to the package directions. If you want to do this step prior to class (and simply have kids decorate signs), then mix and pour the plaster into the cups filling them nearly full. When the plaster thickens after several minutes, poke a dowel rod in each cup.

Explain to kids that they will be making nifty traffic signs to remind us how God guides us—just as traffic signs do when people are walking or driving. Challenge kids to think about how God guides us, then decide which kind of traffic sign they can make to symbolize how God guides and directs us. Mix and pour the plaster if you haven't already done so. Poke the dowel rods into the plaster as it thickens.

As the plaster dries, trace the sign patterns onto poster board and cut them out. Choose the verse strip that accompanies the traffic sign as follows:

- John 14:6 (one way)
- Romans 14:13 (stop sign)
- Matthew 8:13 (go sign)
- Matthew 4:19 (yield sign)

Then have kids use markers and glitter glue to embellish their traffic signs. When the signs are completed, tape them to the top ends of the dowel rods. Tell kids they can place these neat signs in their rooms or around their homes as reminders of how God directs and guides their lives each day.

MAKING THE POINT

Stand the traffic signs around the room, then gather kids at one end of the classroom. Have kids form pairs and explain that they must walk around the room, obeying the traffic signs by reading the verses until they make their way to the opposite end of the room. Tell kids they must visit each traffic sign at least one time before continuing to the end of their goal.

When everyone has traveled to reach the opposite end of the room, ask:

- How are God's directions for our lives like traffic signs?
- What happens if we fail to obey the directions God gives us?
- What roles do faith and trust play in obeying God's directions?
- What can you do this week to obey God's directions and seek His guidance more fully?

Read aloud Psalms 25:5 and 43:3. Briefly discuss what these two important verses teach us about relying on God's direction to guide our lives. End by sharing a prayer thanking God for providing us perfect signs and directions to steer our lives by.

"I am the way and the truth and the life..." (John 14:6)

"Let us stop passing judgment on one another..." (Romans 14:13)

"Go! It will be done just as you believed it would." (Matthew 8:13)

"Come, follow me...and I will make you fishers of men." (Matthew 4:19)

Sudz-n-Dudz

Ezekiel 36:29; 2 Timothy 2:20, 21

God's Power...

Simple Supplies

- tulle or fine netting
- small sandwich bags
- rubber bands
- curling ribbon
- scissors
- powdered bubble bath
- ⅓-cup measuring cup
- tape or a stapler
- copies of the verse cards from page 31 (one per child)

MAKING THE CRAFT

Before class, cut tulle or fine netting into 8-inch squares, one per person. Photocopy the verse cards on page 31, one per person, then cut out the cards. You may wish to pre-cut curling ribbon into 12-inch lengths and curl the ribbons. Be sure you have a rubber band for each person.

Hand each person a small sandwich bag, a square of netting, a rubber band, a verse card, and a length of ribbon. Help kids each measure one-third cup of powdered bubble bath into small sandwich bags. Demonstrate how to place the bag of bubble bath in the center of a square of netting, then pull the four corners up over the bag (to wrap the bags of bubble bath on the netting). Securely fasten a rubber band around the four corners of the netting, then tie a length of ribbon over the rubber band.

Finally, tape or staple a verse card to each ribbon.

MAKING THE POINT

After your craft projects are complete, gather kids and ask them how our bodies can become clean or how we become clean on the outside. Suggestions might include by showers, baths, with soap, or by wearing clean clothing. Then ask:

- In what ways does God make us clean on the inside?
- How does God's forgiveness and salvation through Jesus cleanse us?
- Can we be truly clean without God's salvation through Jesus? Explain.
- In what ways does God's salvation affect our lives? affect our faith?

Invite volunteers to read aloud Ezekiel 36:29 and 2 Timothy 2:20, 21. Then discuss why it's important to be made clean and to receive God's forgiveness through Jesus. Tell kids that their Sudz-n-Dudz can be used to clean bodies in a bath or even clothing in a washer, but that nothing and no one can offer the salvation and cleansing that God offers through His Son, Jesus! Share a prayer thanking God for His cleansing, love and forgiveness. (This may be a great time to invite a church leader in to share about accepting Jesus into kids' lives and hearts!)

TERRIFIC TIP!

Let kids make two Sudz-n-Dudz projects—one to keep and one to share with a family member, friend, or missionary your church sponsors!

 "I will save you from all your uncleanness." —Ezekiel 36:29

 "I will save you from all your uncleanness." —Ezekiel 36:29

 "I will save you from all your uncleanness." —Ezekiel 36:29

 "I will save you from all your uncleanness." —Ezekiel 36:29

The Prayer Trellis
Exodus 22:27; Psalm 10:17

God's Power... Hears our prayers

Simple Supplies

- 6-foot wooden trellises (1 for every 2 kids or 1 trellis per class)
- a roll of white shelf paper
- colored markers
- clear packing tape
- a stapler
- poster board
- scissors
- string (optional)
- crayons (optional)

MAKING THE CRAFT

Before class, cut a wooden trellis in half for every two kids (you may wish to sand any rough edges of plan to have kids do the sanding). If you plan on having one trellis for the entire class, omit the cutting. Cut a length of white shelf paper to line the back of each trellis. Staple the paper in place on the trellis backs. (Again, if you plan on one trellis for the class, you'll only need to attach a large portion of shelf paper on the back of a whole trellis.) Be sure you have a good selection of colorful markers.

Hand each person a trellis half. Briefly discuss the things we might pray for. Suggestions may include prayers for healing of relatives or friends, prayers for the peace of countries of the world, prayers for our pets or family members, prayers for your church or church leaders, or prayers for help in school, with relationships, or other worries and concerns.

Direct children to write brief prayer requests in the spaces between the wooden trellis slats. Suggest that kids also illustrate some of the spaces with colorful designs that remind them of God's power, peace, love, and promises. Stars, hearts, sun shapes, or happy faces make bright designs kids may wish to use. (Leave some of the spaces blank to add prayer requests at home.)

Finally, have kids cut a long rectangular title board to attach to the Prayer Trellis tops. Using markers, have kids write "Prayer Trellis" on their title boards, then attach them to the tops of the trellises using staples or clear packing tape.

MAKING THE POINT

After the projects are completed, invite willing children to share the prayer requests and pictures on their Prayer Trellises. Remind kids that God hears every prayer we pray, no matter when we approach Him—day or night. When everyone who cares to share has had a turn, ask:

- In what ways does God demonstrate His love for us by listening to our prayers?
- Can we be sure that God hears us? Explain.
- Can we be sure that God will answer our prayers? Explain.

Remind kids that, because god loves us and cares for us, He promises to hear our prayers and answer them—even when it may seem as if God isn't listening. Explain that we may not always see God at work, but by faith, we know God is listening and answering. Remind children that God answers our prayers in His own time and in the way He chooses that will be best for us. Explain that when we keep our eyes and hearts open, we see how god hears and answers our prayers, and that the Prayer trellises are great reminders that God's love is always at work for us.

TERRIFIC TIP! Kids love tying a long strings, with a marker or crayon tied to one end, on their Prayer Trellises to add short prayers, praises, and pictures at home!

Invite a volunteer to read aloud Exodus 22:27b and Psalm 10:17. Then ask:

- What are things we can pray for? Who are people we can pray for?
- How can we thank God for listening to and answering our prayers?

Challenge kids to set their Prayer Trellises in a place in their homes where their family members can add their own prayer requests and praises. Then check often to see how God continues to answer those prayers!

Lovin' Those Details!
Matthew 6:25-34

God's Power... Takes care of the details

Simple Supplies

- construction paper (in light colors such as yellow, white, pink, or light blue)
- fine-tipped, permanent black markers
- colored markers
- magnifying glass
- colored ink pads
- a pan of soapy water
- paper towels
- newspapers

MAKING THE CRAFT

Before class, cover a table with newspapers. Set out light-colored construction paper, colored ink pads, fine-tipped permanent markers, and colored markers. (If you wish to make your own "ink" pads, place several paper towels on a paper plate and pour a small spoonful of colored tempera paint in the center of the paper towels, letting the paint soak into the towels. Repeat this for each color of "ink" you desire.)

Demonstrate how to press one of your fingertips onto an ink pad (or paint pad) and firmly press it onto a sheet of construction paper. Slightly roll your fingertip back and forth, then lift it straight upward from the paper to avoid smearing the print. Invite kids to make fingerprints on their papers, using all ten fingers and thumbs.

When the prints are made, invite kids to notice the details in the fingerprints. Then challenge kids to add their own details to make mini pictures using their fingerprints. Suggest making cute mice, bears, fish, birds, flowers, or other simple designs by adding details using the fine-tipped permanent markers.

When the details have been added, finish by having kids use colored makers to add colors to their drawings if desired.

MAKING THE POINT

Pass around a magnifying glass and let kids look closely at the details of their own fingertips and fingerprints. As you pass the glass, discuss how each person's fingerprints are unique and hold special details that are only found in that one person. Remind kids that God is our Creator and that He alone designed the details we see in our fingerprints. Ask:

- How do our fingerprints demonstrate God's attention to detail?
- What other details has God put into His creation of people, animals, plants, and the rest of the heavens and earth?
- How does it help to know that God cares and provides for even the smallest details in our lives?
- In what ways does God's attention to the smallest details demonstrate His love for us?

Remind kids that God doesn't leave anything to chance—He plans and carries out His will in each detail, and He provides for us even in the smallest of ways. Invite children to take turns reading aloud the passage from Matthew 6:25-34. Discuss the different ways this passage tells us that God provides for His creation. Point out that since God provides for us in every way, we don't need to worry about large or small concerns. Then ask:

- Why is it silly to worry about things when God is in control?
- Who is better able to handle everything: God or us? Explain.
- How can we trust God more, knowing He provides for the tiniest details of our lives?

Let children make a heart shape on their papers, then make a fingerprint over the heart. Add the words: "God is in the details!" Challenge kids to look for the ways God provides for us through His loving attention to details each day.

Fitting-Plans Serving Bowl

Proverbs 23:18; Jeremiah 29:11

God's Power... Promises us a future

Simple Supplies

- an 8-inch plastic bowl for each person
- self-hardening tub caulk
- ceramic or glass tiles in a variety of shapes and colors (available in bulk from craft stores)
- fine-tipped permanent black marker or black paint pens
- damp paper towels
- newspapers
- craft sticks or plastic knives

MAKING THE CRAFT

Before class, purchase bulk bags of small ceramic or glass tiles and shapes. These are available at most craft stores and have smoothed edges for safety—although you'll want to caution kids to be careful when handling the tiles. (If you have younger kids, consider using large plastic jewels, buttons, or metal nuts and bolts instead of glass tiles.) Make a bowl to show kids as a sample.

Spread newspapers on a table and set out the ceramic or glass tiles, tubes of tub caulk, craft sticks or plastic knives, and paint pens or permanent markers.

Hand each person a plastic bowl. Demonstrate how to squeeze a bead of tub caulk around a portion of the bowl's top edge (work on small sections of the edge, one section at a time). Fit ceramic or glass tile and shapes into the caulk around the edges of the 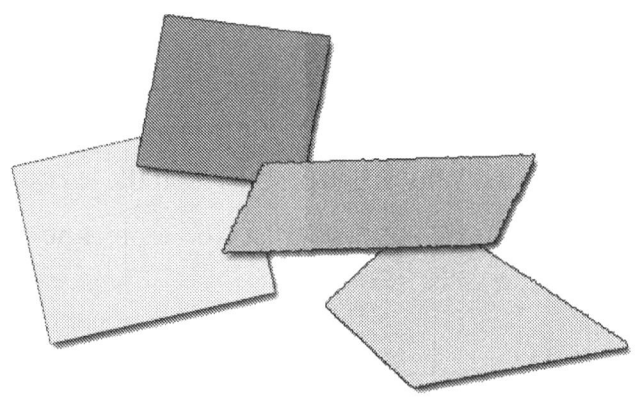 bowls. Kids may make as wide an edge as they desire, but be sure to continue the entire way around the top edge of each bowl.

As kids work, make comments such as, "You need to carefully plan how you will fit all the pieces in" and "Each piece has its own shape and size, doesn't it? It can be a challenge to fit the pieces together in a pleasing way!"

When the edges of the bowls are covered in tiles mosaic-style, have kids use fine-tipped permanent black markers or black paint pens to write Jeremiah 29:1 on the sides of the bowls. Write:

"For I know the plans I have for you" Jeremiah 29:11.

When kids are finished writing, set aside the bowls to dry. Point out that when the caulk is completely dry (tomorrow), the bowls can be used to serve chips, breads, crackers, or other dry snacks in. Tell kids to hand wash the bowls when they need cleaning or simply wipe them off using a damp cloth.

TRY THIS!
Glue jigsaw puzzle pieces instead of using caulk and tiles around the edge of bowls. Add spray lacquer to make the bowls more water resistant (hand wash only).

MAKING THE POINT

As the bowls dry, gather kids and briefly discuss how making plans helps us accomplish goals, plan for fun, and generally helps us get through each day in positive ways. Then ask:

- ✂ In what ways is fitting plans together like fitting pieces into the serving bowls we just made?

- ✂ Do our plans always work out the way we'd like? Explain.

- ✂ Is it possible for us to control, think of, or change every detail in our plans to make sure they go smoothly? Explain.

Remind kids that we are only in control of our own actions and responses—and that only God is in ultimate control. Explain that God's perfect plans for us always have a way of working out as He desires—as long as we are obedient, seek His will, and follow God's plans. And even though there are loads of details in God's plans, we can trust they will work out as He desires.

Invite volunteers to read aloud Jeremiah 29:11 and Proverbs 23:18. Discuss how God's plans provide hope and assurance for a bright future. Remind kids that God even planned for us to be forgiven through sending His Son, Jesus Christ, to die for our sins!

End by sharing a prayer and thanking God for promising us a future through His perfect plans and will. Challenge kids to remember God's powerful promise each time they use their serving bowls and see the way the pieces fit around the edges, just as God fits together the details of His plans for our lives. Invite kids to remind their friends and family members that God has a plan for their lives as well!

Rock-Solid Forgiveness
Psalm 18:2; Matthew 6:14, 15; Romans 4:7

God's Power...

Forgives us

Simple Supplies

- large, flat stones (one per person)
- tacky craft glue
- craft felt (in a variety of colors)
- scissors
- paint pens
- glitter glue
- sequins
- plastic jewels

MAKING THE CRAFT

Before class, make sure you have a large, flat stone (smooth surfaces) for each child. Flat garden cobbles work especially well for this craft project.

Set out the craft materials and hand each person a flat stone or cobble. Have kids cut a piece of craft felt (either a circle or square shape) to fit the bottom of the stones. Use tacky craft glue to attach the felt shapes on the bottom surfaces of the stones. Explain that the felt will protect tables or desks from being scratched when you place the stone on them. As you work, challenge kids to think about how God forgives us when we need to be forgiven. Point out that God covers, forgives, and protects us as the felt protects tabletops from any scratches we may inadvertently make with the stones. Ask kids to describe how God's forgiveness feels. Suggestions might include "God's forgiveness gives us life," "God's forgiveness shows His love," or "Being forgiven means being loved!"

Next, invite kids to use the paint pens to write a short note about God's forgiving love or Jesus' forgiveness in their lives. Then embellish the stones using glitter glue, sequins, plastic jewels, and scraps of craft felt.

When the Forgiveness Stones are finished, set them aside to

dry completely. These special stones can then be used as paper weights, table decorations, or desk ornaments to remind kids of the rock-solid love God provides us through His forgiveness!

MAKING THE POINT

As the Forgiveness Stones are drying, gather kids and briefly discuss times kids needed to be forgiven at home or in school and how it felt. Encourage kids to express how it feels to need forgiveness and receive it. Remind kids that we all need forgiveness for careless or hurtful things we say and do, but that we also need forgiveness from God for times we disobey Him or do the things God tells us are wrong—which is called *sin*. Remind kids that the Bible tells us we have all sinned and fallen short of God's glory—and that we all need God's forgiveness to live close to Him. Ask:

- **How is God's forgiveness a demonstration of His deep love for us?**
- **In what ways does receiving God's forgiveness help us draw closer to God?**
- **How does it affect the way we think, act, and treat others when we know we're forgiven?**

Remind kids that God's supreme act of forgiving us was sending His Son, Jesus, to die for our sins so we could live with God forever! When we ask for God's forgiveness, it is brought to us through Jesus and through accepting Jesus into our lives. Invite volunteers to read aloud Psalm 18:2; Matthew 6:14, 15; and Romans 4:7. Briefly discuss how God desires us to forgive others as He has forgiven us. Then ask:

- **Why do you think God desires us to forgive others?**
- **How does being willing to forgive others pass along God's rock-solid love to others?**
- **Why are we blessed when we receive God's forgiveness? when we offer forgiveness to others?**

Tell kids that God's love is rock solid because it never changes nor can it be shaken, crumbled, or changed. Point out that God's forgiveness is the same way. Through His power to forgive us, God has given us second chances at obeying Him as He desires—and the gift of offering our forgiveness to others who need it. End by sharing a prayer thanking God for His power to forgive us and to help us forgive others.

> **TRY THIS!**
> Bring in a stone large enough to stand on. Point out how a rock doesn't crumble or falter when we put our weight on it—and this is how God's forgiveness is. God's love and forgiveness stand firm even under the weight of our sins.

Prayer Pockets
Proverbs 3:5, 6; Jeremiah 33:3

God's Power...

Simple Supplies

- wall paper samples
- scissors
- a stapler
- photocopies of the verse card from page 41
- markers
- self-adhesive hook-and-loop fasteners
- craft glue
- 2-by-3-inch slips of paper
- small pencils, pens, or markers (one per child)

MAKING THE CRAFT

Before class, cut pages from a wall paper samples book. You'll need an 8-by-10-inch (or larger) sample page for each person. Cut out more pages than you'll need so kids will have a choice of which papers they like. Make photocopies of the verse card from page 41, one copy per person.

Invite kids to choose the wall paper patterns they like. Demonstrate how to fold the sample pages in half lengthwise, then staple up the open sides leaving the top edges open. This will make the pages into long "pockets." Encourage kids to work in pairs and to help one another.

When the sides of the pockets are stapled, have kids trim the verse cards then glue them in place on the pocket fronts. Invite kids to color the verse cards or the wall paper patterns using markers if they wish.

hook-n-loop fastener

Show kids how to apply self-adhesive hook-and-loop fasteners to the inside center edges of the pocket openings. Hand each child several slips of paper and a small pencil, pen, or marker to place inside of his or her Prayer Pocket. Tell kids you will explain how the Prayer Pockets work in a moment. Finally, invite kids to use markers to write their names on the backs of their Prayer Pockets.

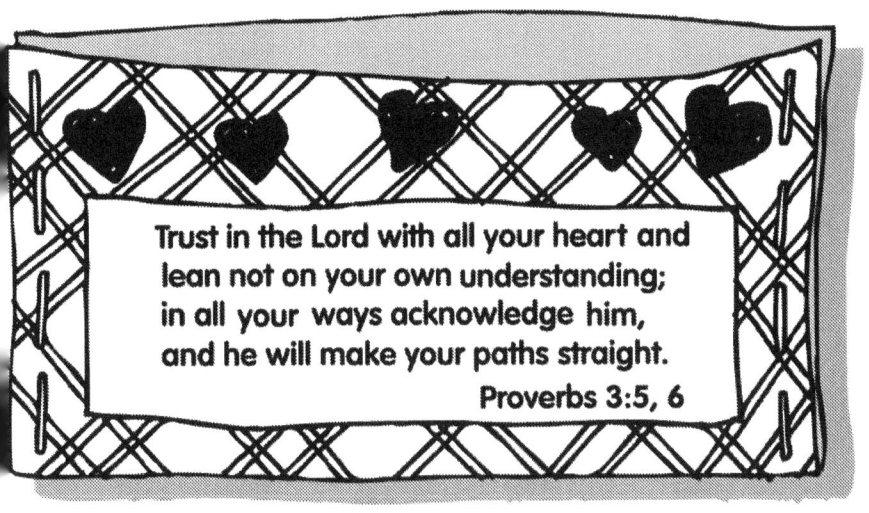

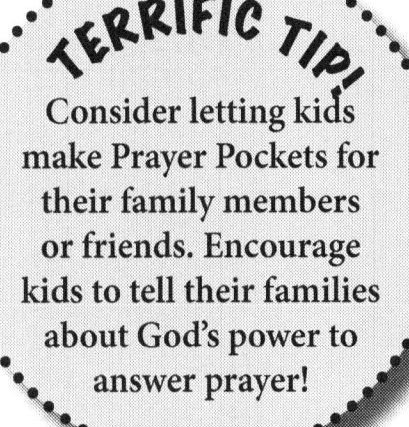

MAKING THE POINT

Ask kids to tell about times they've prayed and God has answered those prayers. Encourage everyone to tell how it felt to know that God had heard and answered their prayers. Remind kids that God promises to hear us—and to answer each and every prayer in His own time and way. Explain that the Prayer Pockets can help kids take note of when and how God answers their prayers. Have kids write short prayers, needs, and requests to God on one side of each slip of paper, then tuck those papers in their Prayer Pockets. As prayers are answered, have kids write how God answered on the backs of the corresponding slips of paper.

Read aloud Proverbs 3:5, 6 and Jeremiah 33:3. Discuss how trusting in God to answer our prayers gives us strength and wisdom. Point out that when we trust God to answer our needs and worries, things have the perfect way of working out! Remind kids that it often takes patience to trust in God's timing—but that God promises to answer every prayer in the ways that are best for us.

"Trust in the Lord with all your heart and lean not on your own understanding; in all your ways acknowledge him, and he will make your paths straight."

—Proverbs 3:5, 6

The Ring of Victory!
Philippians 2:10, 11; 1 Corinthians 15:57

God's Power...

Gives us victory

Simple Supplies

- a key ring for each child
- colored beading wire (in a variety of colors)
- alphabet pony beads
- solid-colored pony beads
- fine-tipped black permanent markers
- needle-nosed pliers (several pairs)
- wire cutters

MAKING THE CRAFT

Before class, make sure you have enough letter beads to spell out Jesus' name for each child. If you need to make additional letter beads, write the letters using a fine-tipped, black permanent marker on solid-colored pony beads. (Older kids will enjoy choosing their own colors of beads and writing the letters themselves.) You may wish to cut varying lengths of colorful beading wire before class. Cut lengths from 4-inches to 6-inches. Plan on having several pairs of needle-nosed pliers available as kids will be using them to bend the wires around the key rings.

Set out the beads, colored wire, and needle-nosed pliers. Hand each person a key ring. Demonstrate how to take a length of wire and, using the pliers, bend and twist the wire into interesting shapes. Then make a loop at one end of the wire and thread the loop through the key ring. Have kids make several of these bent wires. (Kids may wish to thread small beads on the wires, but tell them not to use the letter beads yet.)

Demonstrate how to make a loop at one end of a wire, then thread letter beads (in reverse order) to spell out Jesus' name. Make another loop at the top end of the wire to attach it to the key ring (see illustration).

Tell kids that there is glorious power in the name of Jesus—and that God gives us ultimate victory over sin and eternal death through His Son, Jesus! Explain that these special key rings can be used for keys, hooked onto the zippers of jackets or backpacks, or hung from a chain and suspended in windows.

TERRIFIC TIP!

Placing small beads in muffin tins keep the colors separated and at kids' fingertips!

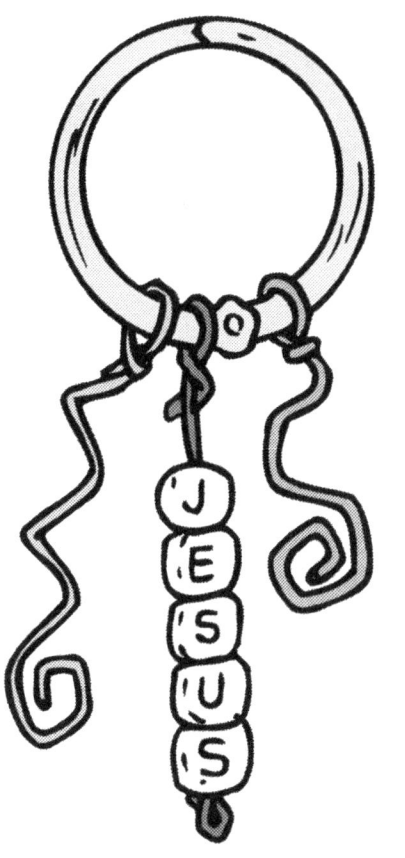

MAKING THE POINT

After kids have finished making their special key rings, have them sit in a circle holding their projects. Have the fine-tipped, black permanent markers handy as you'll be adding a verse reference to the backs of the beads in a few moments. Ask:

- ✄ What name is spelled out on your key rings?
- ✄ Why do you think that Jesus' name is the most special name under heaven?

Briefly discuss how God sent Jesus to be our savior—to save us from sin and eternal death. Invite volunteers to read aloud 1 Corinthians 15:57, then ask:

- ✄ What victory do we have in Jesus?
- ✄ In what ways does God's power give us victory through Jesus?

Remind kids that before God sent His precious Son, we lived in the darkness of sin, eternal death, and we were unforgiven. But through God's incredible love for us, His Son, Jesus, died for our sins so we could receive forgiveness and live in harmony with God eternally. Remind kids that the gift of God's salvation through Jesus is for everyone who asks Jesus into their lives, receives His forgiveness, and calls upon the name of Jesus to guide their lives.

Invite a volunteer to read aloud Philippians 2:10, 11. Then ask:

- ✄ **In what ways does calling upon the name of Jesus draw us closer to God?**
- ✄ **What other power does the name of Jesus bring to our lives besides forgiveness and salvation?**
- ✄ **How can we thank God for the gift of Jesus?**

Remind kids that we call upon the powerful name of Jesus when we have worries, when we're weary or feel discouraged, when we feel alone, or any time we want the power and strength of Jesus to help in our lives or in the lives of people we love. Have kids use the fine-tipped, black permanent markers to write on the backs of the letter beads of their key rings as follows (to signify Philippians 2:10, 11):

Bead 1 (top bead): the letter P
Bead 2: the number 2
Bead 3: a colon
Bead 4: the number 10
Bead 5: the number 11

No Eggheads Here!
Proverbs 2:6, 3:13, 8:11

God's Power...
Gives us wisdom

Simple Supplies

- paper or foam egg cartons
- scissors
- permanent markers (black and various colors)
- potting soil
- plastic pull-apart eggs
- plastic spoons
- newspapers
- grass seeds

MAKING THE CRAFT

Collect the craft materials including the paper or foam egg cartons, scissors, permanent markers, potting soil, spoons, grass seeds, and plastic pull-apart eggs (or real egg shell halves). Cover a table with newspaper and spread out the materials. Before class, make sure you've cut apart the egg cups so there's one cup per person.

Hand each child a paper or foam egg cup. Invite kids to decorate the egg cups leaving one side blank so that words can be added later. Designs that work well include stars, hearts, simple flowers, or polka dots.

Glue the egg shell halves (plastic or real) into the cups, then use permanent markers to add facial features to one side of the eggs.

When the faces are added, demonstrate how to scoop potting soil into the egg shell halves until about a half inch from the top. Scatter grass seeds on the soil, then scoop more soil into the cups to cover the seeds. Pour a bit of water on to settle the soil and moisten the seeds. Explain to kids that in a couple of weeks, if the eggheads are kept moist and placed in a sunny location in their homes, the grass will grow and look like hair! Tell kids they can trim the grassy hair in any style they'd like.

MAKING THE POINT

After your craft projects are complete, set them aside. You'll be writing a Scripture verse on the egg cups shortly, so keep the fine-tipped permanent black markers handy. Gather kids and ask:

- What kinds of things do we fill our minds with each day?
- How does what we put into our minds affect what comes out in our hearts, words, and actions?

Say: **We spend our time filling our minds with everything from worries and facts we learn at school, to music, movies, video games, the Internet, and television shows. And each time we put into our minds affects us in some way. If we stop to consider for a moment, we might just discover that what we fill our heads and minds with comes out in our hearts, words, and actions. If we fill ourselves with negative thoughts and feelings, if we spend too much time listening to music with negative lyrics or watching movies with violent themes, we become less sensitive, kind, and thoughtful.** Ask:

- What do you think God wants us to fill our minds with?
- How is God's wisdom the best thing to fill our minds with?
- What can having God's wisdom do for us?

Invite volunteers to read aloud Proverbs 2:6, 12; 3:13; 4:5, 7; and 8:11. Say: **God's Word tells us over and over again to get wisdom—to fill our minds, hearts, and lives with wisdom based in God's own Word. When we seek God's wisdom by reading and learning His Word in the Bible, we can avoid sin, temptation, making wrong choices, and disobeying God. Wisdom teaches us how to live in peace with others and draw closer to God. Wisdom helps us make good decisions that are in line with what God desires. When we forget to fill our minds with wisdom from God, we become real eggheads! Let's write a short verse about wisdom on our eggheads as reminders of the importance of seeking God's wisdom in our lives—and so we won't become hollow eggheads!**

Have kids us fine-tipped permanent black markers to write the following on their egg cups: *"Blessed is he who finds wisdom" Proverbs 3:13."*

> **TERRIFIC TIP!**
> Try using quick-germinating flower seeds such as marigolds instead of grass—or try radish seeds!

3-in-1 to Overcome!
Job 12:13; Colossians 1:13, 14; Romans 15:13

Simple Supplies

- individually-wrapped lollipops (3 per person)
- scissors
- rubber bands
- ribbon
- googly eyes
- black permanent markers
- tape
- photocopies of the three cards from page 47

MAKING THE CRAFT

Collect the craft materials including scissors, rubber bands, tape, curling ribbon, small googly eyes, craft glue or glue sticks, and black permanent markers or black paint pens. Be sure you have three, individually-wrapped lollipops for each child. Photocopy the verse cards from the facing page, one set of three cards for each person. Cut out the cards (or have older kids cut out their own cards).

Invite kids to work with partners as they prepare their lollipop bouquets. Glue a pair of googly eyes on each lollipop and use permanent markers to add noses and mouths, hair, or other desired features.

When the lollipop faces are finished, show kids how to wrap rubber bands around the lollipop sticks to join the pops into a bouquet. Tie curling ribbon around the rubber bands. Finally, have kids tape a verse card to each lollipop stick.

If you have extra lollipops and supplies, let your kids make a bouquet (or even individual lollipops) with faces and verse cards to share with kids in another class. These cute lollies make good party favors, package toppers, or simple serving gifts for members of the church congregation, too!

MAKING THE POINT

When the lollipop bouquets are complete, gather kids and ask them what kinds of things might be displeasing to God. Suggestions might include hurtful words, sin, and disobeying God. Say: **The Bible tells us there are many things that cause God to become sad or angry. Sin and disobedi-**

ence are two of the worst—and we know we've all sinned because the Bible tells us so. We've all felt temptation to say or do something God tells us is wrong. So how do we fight evil, temptation, and sin? How do we overcome disobedience to God? We need help! And our loving God has provided that help for us in the form of the Trinity! God, His Son, Jesus, and the Holy Spirit are joined in God's power to help us overcome all evil in the world.

Invite volunteers to read aloud the following verses: *Job 12:13* (God's power), *Colossians 1:13, 14* (Christ's forgiveness), and *Romans 15:13* (hope by the Holy Spirit). Then ask:

- In what ways does Jesus help us overcome sin?
- How can the Holy Spirit help us overcome temptation and follow God more closely?

Say: **Isn't it wonderful the way has supplied for us to overcome evil. God, our Father, is all-powerful. We can trust Him and know that what God tells us is the absolute truth. God's power is perfect and God is in control. God's power helps us overcome evil. God gave us His only Son, Jesus, to forgive our sins and make us new creations who live closer to God. And Jesus sent us the Holy Spirit to be our friend and special helper to keep us on the straight path to God. When we rely on the power of God, Jesus, and the Holy Spirit, we can overcome evil, sin, and temptations—and there's nothing sweeter than that—not even our lollipop bouquets!**

God's Power

Jesus' Forgiveness

The Holy Spirit's Help

SECTION 2: OBJECT TALKS

Object talks are the most flexible, nutritious teaching tools you'll ever *love!*

Matching up everyday items, objects, foods, and more with biblical themes creates some of the quickest and most memorable messages you'll ever impart to kids of any age. Focus on a biblical theme or choose one you're working on in class, then match up an object talk from this section, and you're on the way to filling each moment with memorable learning fun. And many of the terrific talks included here have lively projects for kids to make-n-do—then carry home to share with their families!

Kids love lively messages!

Each memorable message included in *20/20 Crafts & Object Talks That Teach About God's Power* offers solid, Bible-based learning in the form of lively object talks using simple, everyday-type items. Every object talk is based on an attribute of God's power to help kids know, love, and obey God more closely while building their faith in God's perfect plans and power. Use these quick object talks to enrich a Bible lesson you're learning, reinforce what kids are discovering about God's power, or to accompany specific Scripture verses. You'll find a handy *Activities and Themes Index* at the back of the book to help you match up crafts, object talks, and themes—and the *Contents* page lists the various Scripture verses used in each object talk.

From balls to birthday cakes, objects and interesting items make Bible messages memorable in fun—and often festive—ways!

Have fun teaching your kids about God's perfect power through these awesome object talks—and watch the smiles *and* your kids' faith grow!

Here and Back Prayers
Psalms 34:4, 118:21; Jeremiah 33:3

God's Power...
Answers our prayers

Simple Supplies

- scissors
- markers
- crayons
- photocopies of the earth and rocket picture on page 51 (one per child plus one extra)
- aluminum foil (optional)
- glitter glue (optional)
- craft glue (optional)

PREPARING THE TALK

Before class, photocopy the earth and rocket picture from page 51 making a copy for yourself and one for each child. Cut the pictures on the dotted line to separate them from the rest of the page. Place the papers on a table along with markers and crayons kids can use to color the pictures later. (You may wish to include bits of shiny aluminum foil and craft glue or glitter glue to embellish the pictures.) Before the presentation you'll also want to practice with the picture a few times. Hold the paper so the star shape is touching your nose. Turn the page around slowly to the left (counter clockwise). As you slowly rotate the paper, you'll see that the rocket flies away from the earth, then lands again! Practice this illusion several times until you're familiar with how it works. Kids will be launching and landing their own rockets using these papers during message time.

PRESENTING THE POINT

Gather kids in front of you. Invite everyone to tell about a time he or she prayed and how God answered those prayers. Encourage kids to express how it felt to have their prayers answered. Remind kids that God listens every time we pray because he loves us, wants to help us, and cares about all we have to say to Him.

Distribute the rocket papers and tell kids that you have a nifty things for them to watch. Show kids how to place the stars on their papers on their noses and rotate the papers to make the rockets fly away and land again. Let kids help one another if someone has trouble viewing the launch and landing of his rocket.

After everyone has seen the rockets fly away and return, ask:

✂ In what ways is a rocket ship like prayers we send to God?

✂ How do we know our prayers reach God?

✂ Why do you suppose God sends His answers back to us?

Explain that when we pray, our requests, petitions, worries, praises, and thank you's all travel at lightning-fast speeds to God—and God promises to hear and answer each prayer in His time and way. Invite a volunteer to read aloud Jeremiah 33:3 and Psalms 34:4 and 118:21. Then ask:

- ✂ **How do God's answers to prayer demonstrate His great love for us?**

- ✂ **Does God always answer in the ways we want? Explain.**

- ✂ **In what ways does knowing God hears and answers our prayers draw us closer to God and help us trust Him even more?**

Let kids try their rockets again as you remind them that prayers are like fast rockets to God—which are answered and returned to us in God's own time and way. Invite kids to use markers to write a prayer request on the rocket in their picture, then color the shapes as desired. Challenge kids to read their prayer requests to God each day as they wait for God to send them an answer to prayer. Remind kids to be sure and thank God for His love and faithfulness in listening and answering their prayers.

Our prayers launch to God, who hears every prayer we pray.

God answers each prayer and send His answers—in His own time and way—back to us!

Permission to photocopy for church, school, or home use only. Taken from *20/20 Crafts & Object Talks That Teach About God's Power* © Susan Lingo, Susan Lingo Books, 2007.

Resist 'n Run!

1 Peter 3:11; James 4:7, 8

God's Power...

Helps us resist evil

Simple Supplies

- a glass bowl
- water
- pepper shaker
- liquid dish soap
- scissors
- markers
- clear tape
- photocopy of the label from page 53

PREPARING THE TALK

Before class, photocopy the label from page 53 (or make a similar one from construction paper) to tape over the label on a container of liquid dish washing soap. Just prior to presenting your object talk, fill a clear bowl with water. Place the shaker of pepper and the God's Power soap beside the bowl. You may wish to practice this object talk once before presenting it to the class. Simply shake pepper onto the surface of the water until the surface is covered. Then add a few drops of "God's Power" to the center of the water and watch the pepper dots scoot to the sides of the bowl. You'll be adding the pepper and soap during the object talk, so begin with a fresh bowl of water.

PRESENTING THE POINT

Gather kids around the bowl of water. Hold up the pepper and say: **There are many things in this world that are not of God. Hatred, killing, and jealousy are some of those things. Satan goes all around the world looking for ways to sprinkle the world and people with bad things!** Sprinkle pepper in the bowl of water so it covers the top of the surface.

Say: **Evil and temptations to disobey God are real—and Satan is just as real as he goes about looking for ways to accomplish evil, sin, temptation, and disobedience.** Ask:

- What are things that might tempt us to disobey God or His rules?
- Why is disobedience to God a bad choice that can land us in trouble?
- In what ways do sin and disobedience lead us away from God?

Say: **Evil, sin, and temptation are like black spots or stains that can cover our lives and rob us of a relationship with God. They are real—and really bad! We can't fight and resist by our own power—we need *God's power* to help us resist, turn from evil, and stay focused on God!** Hold up the dish washing liquid labeled "God's Power." Say: **When we put God's power to work in our lives** (add a few drops of liquid soap to the center of the pepper in the bowl), **evil, sin, and temptations run like crazy! That's because evil cannot live alongside good, and Satan cannot live in the presence of God or God's perfect power!** Ask:

- What are ways we can put God's power to work in our lives?
- How can relying on God help us steer clear of temptations and resist evil?

Read aloud 1 Peter 3:11, James 4:7, 8 and Job 12:13. Discuss ways to resist evil and how trusting in God's power can help us overcome temptations that may come our way. End with a prayer thanking God for His ultimate power to give victory to good over evil.

Superbly Surrounded
Psalms 32:10, 125:2

God's Power... Surrounds us

Simple Supplies
- index cards
- scissors

PREPARING THE TALK

Before class, collect index cards and a pair of scissors for each child or every two kids. Practice the folding and cutting directions for the index cards before presenting this object talk. This slick trick is awesome and provides amazing results that kids will love—and it's easy to do once you know how!

To make a step-through index card, simply fold an index card in half lengthwise, then cut nearly through the cards at half-inch intervals (see figure A in the margin). Repeat the cutting process from the other side of the card, cutting between your first cuts almost to the edge of the card (refer to figure B). Finally, open the card carefully and cut down the center of the card without cutting the first or last strips on either end of the card (see figure C). Then slowly stretch out the cut card and voilà—slip the card over your head and carefully step through the index card (figure D on opposite page)!

A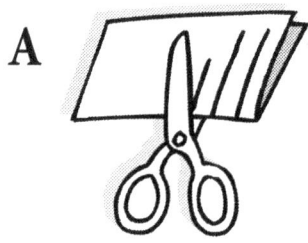

B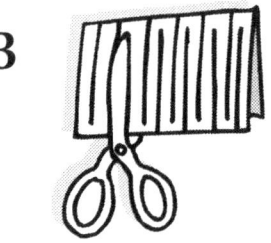

C

PRESENTING THE POINT

Hold an index card and a pair of scissors. Gather kids on the floor in front of you. Say: **I'm holding a small card commonly called and "index card." These nifty cards are useful for writing notes on, using them for bookmarks, or great for recipes. But do you think an index card would be good for surrounding someone like a blanket? Could an index card even be large enough to completely surround a person?** Let kids share their thoughts and ideas. Encourage them to tell why it would seem impossible for an index card to surround something or someone. Then say: **Sometimes an idea seems impossible. But is it really impossible for a small index card to stretch enough to surround me? Let's see!**

As you cut the index card and prepare it for stepping through, discuss what it means to surround something—to be all around something or someone at one time. Encourage kids to tell if they think it's possible for a human to cover or surround someone completely, all the time, in every way and why or why not. When you're ready to stretch the index card, say: **Are you ready to see if this one small card can be all around me at one time? Here we go!** Slowly and carefully stretch the card so it surrounds you—then pause and step through the card. Say: **What a cool trick! We accomplished what seemed impossible. We may need tricks to accomplish the impossible, but God doesn't! Remember, God's power is ultimate so the impossible *is* possible! An index card isn't really capable of surrounding us completely or protecting and covering us all the time and wherever we go—but God is.** Ask:

- ✂ How was this like being surrounded by God's presence?
- ✂ Is it possible to be surrounded by God's power, grace, love, forgiveness, and protection all the time? Explain.
- ✂ How does it strengthen our faith to know that God and His power completely surround us all the time—no matter where we are or what we're facing?

Invite volunteers to read aloud Psalms 32:10 and 125:2. Remind kids that because of God's great power and love, we can be assured He is all around us, surrounding us with His strength. Lead kids in how to do this simple trick so they can show their families and remind them of God's power to surround and cover us.

D

The Sweetest Teacher
Psalm 119:103; 2 Timothy 3:16, 17

God's Power... Teaches us

Simple Supplies

- white plastic spoons
- lemon juice
- white or brown sugar
- a jar of honey
- small, clean jars with lids
- ribbon
- yellow and black permanent markers
- scissors
- tape
- photocopies of the verse on page 57 (one per child)

PREPARING THE TALK

Before class, photocopy the verse box from page 57, one copy per child. These will be labels that will be taped to the sides of small jars later in the object talk. Be sure you have a clean, small jar and lid, and a plastic spoon for each child. You'll also need small amounts of sugar (brown or white), lemon juice, and honey for kids to taste. (You may wish to have enough honey to fill the baby-food jars about three-quarters full for kids to take home to share.) Be sure you have both black and yellow permanent markers for this object talk.

PRESENTING THE POINT

Hand each child a plastic spoon. Tell them they're going to have the chance to taste three food items and must decide which is sweetest. Squirt a drop or two of lemon juice on each spoon and let kids taste the sourness. As them if this food was sweet and if they know what the fruit the juice is from. Then pour a taste of white or brown sugar on each plastic spoon and let kids taste the sugar. Again, invite them to give their reactions to the sweetness and identify what they just tasted. Finally, pour honey on each spoon and let kids test the sweetness against the lemon juice and the sugar. Encourage kids to tell which was least sweet, which was next, and which food was sweetest of all.

Say: **Honey was the sweetest food we tasted—and mmm, it is tasty, isn't it? Some people think honey is the sweetest food God has made! But the Bible tells us there's something even sweeter than honey. Do you know what that is? Let's read a special verse and see if you can discover what is even sweeter than honey.** Invite a volunteer to read aloud Psalm 119:103, then have kids tell that God's Word is sweeter than honey. Ask:

✂ What does the Bible mean when it says that God's Word is sweeter than honey?

✂ How does God's Word teach us? help us draw closer to God? guide us and lead us?

Read aloud 2 Timothy 3:16, 17. Then say: **There is nothing sweeter than the way God's Word teaches us about God, His power, truth, and how to obey Him. And just as honey is good for us and packed with vitamins and minerals, God's Word is nutritious, too! Let's make cute honey jars with bumblebee spoons to remind us how sweet God's Word is.**

For each honey jar, glue a verse label to a small jar. Next, color a plastic spoon to look like a bee as in the illustration. (Fill the honey jars three-quarters full with honey if you have enough), then screw the lids on securely. Tie a ribbon bow around the neck of the honey jar and tape the spoon to the lid. When the honey jars are complete, say: **You can enjoy tasty, nutritious honey with your families and friends as you remind them of the sweet, nutritious nature of God's Word and how it teaches us God's sweet truths!**

How sweet are your words to my taste, sweeter than honey to my mouth! (Psalm 119:103)

Multiply His Love!
Romans 12:10, 13:8; Ephesians 4:2

Simple Supplies

- a roll of white shelf paper
- pencils
- markers
- scissors
- tape (optional)
- glitter glue (optional)

PREPARING THE TALK

Collect the materials in the supplies box. Cut 2-foot lengths of white shelf paper, one per person plus several for yourself. (You'll use one or two long strips to practice with before class.) This object talk is similar to cutting out paper dolls—there will be portions of hearts cut so that when opened, they link together and grow into several hearts.

Practice folding and cutting the hearts before presenting this object talk. To make linked hearts, take a length of white shelf paper and fold it in half lengthwise (see figure A). Fold the rectangle in half again (figure B). Then use a pencil to lightly draw on cutting lines as in illustration C. The lines will form the left and right halves of two hearts. Cut on the dotted lines. Carefully open the cut-out shape to reveal several linked hearts (refer to figure D). During the object talk, you'll

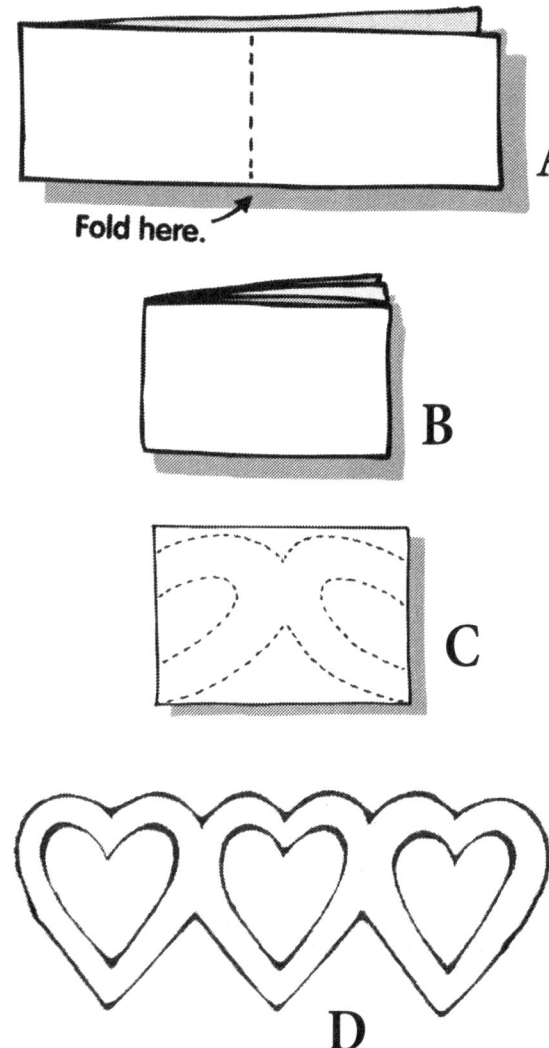

show kids how to fold, draw, and cut out their own linked hearts. Have enough pencils, paper strips, and scissors for kids to cut along with you. You'll need two long, paper strips for yourself. Fold one of the strips and lightly draw on the dotted lines.

PRESENTING THE POINT

Gather kids in front of you. Hold the scissors and long paper strip with the dotted lines. Ask kids how many strips of paper you're holding. Then say: **Let's pretend as if this one heart represents the one heart that began all love. Whose heart do you think that would belong to?** Lead kids to tell that God's heart began all love. Then continue: **God's love folds around us in perfect ways!** (Fold the strip in half.) **God's love folds around us through His forgiveness, patience, mercy, grace, and compassion.** (Fold the strip in half again making sure the dotted lines are showing.) Cut along the dotted lines as you say: **It was God who first loved us and it's God who desires us to spread His love to others—wherever we go. How can we multiply God's love and compassion to other people?** Encourage kids to share their ideas about how we can spread love. When the dotted lines have been cut, slowly open the linked hearts as you say: **Look what happens when we multiply God's love to others…it links us all together! One heart of love multiplies into many, many hearts of love, compassion, and selfless giving. God's love passes to us and from us, to others.**

Invite volunteers to read aloud Romans 12:10, 13:8, and Ephesians 4:2. Then ask:

✂ **Why do you suppose God desires us to spread His love to others?**

✂ **How does sharing God's love draw us closer to one another? closer to God?**

✂ **Can a strong link of love with God at the center be easily broken? Explain.**

Hand out the long strips of paper, pencils, and scissors. Hold the other long strip you have and lead kids in folding, drawing the half hearts, and cutting on the dotted lines to make their own linked hearts. Then use markers to write "We can multiply God's love powerfully to other people" around the lower edges of the linked hearts. Embellish the tops of the hearts with glitter glue if desired. You may wish to have kids color the linked hearts, then tape them all together for a great classroom display of love!

Forever Forgiven
Psalm 103:12; Romans 4:7; Colossians 1:13, 14

God's Power...

Simple Supplies

- a sliding match box
- index card
- clear tape
- glue stick
- scissors
- fine-tipped marker

PREPARING THE TALK

Before class, prepare a secret sliding match box by cutting a small rectangle from an index card to fit across the center of the bottom of the match box (see illustration A).

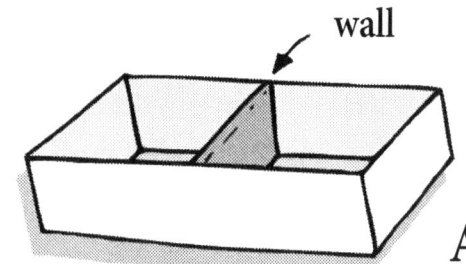

A

Next, cover the top of the match box with a rectangle cut from the index card. Glue on the cover with a glue stick. Decorate the cover with heart shapes or stickers (illustration B). Cut a small rectangular card to fit inside one half of the bottom box. Use a fine-tipped marker to write the words "Stealing and lying" on the card, then place the card in on half of the bottom box (figure B).

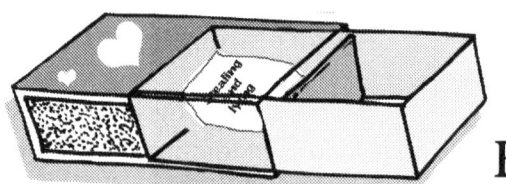

B

During the object talk, you'll read the card to the kids, then place it in the box. When you slyly turn the box around in your hand and push the bottom box outward halfway, it will be empty and appear as if the card just disappeared (figure C)! Try this trick several times before class to become comfortable with how it works.

C

TERRIFIC TIP!

It's important to remember which end the card is hidden in the secret box so you don't push out the wrong end! Be sure to practice before class.

PRESENTING THE POINT

Hold the secret match box in one hand and the small index card in the other hand. Ask kids to tell about times they needed forgiveness for something they said or did. Encourage them to express how it felt to be forgiven. Then say: **There are so many times we need to be forgiven—and we all have needed forgiveness at some time! Maybe we said hurtful things to a friend or treated someone in a rude way. These are small acts of unkindness that need forgiving, but there are bigger disobedient things people say and do which God tells us is** *sin*.

Hold up the small card and read the words "stealing and lying." Say: **Let's say that this card represents things we need forgiveness for. I'll place it in this special box as we read some verses about forgiveness from God's Word.** Place the card in the box (remember which end it is on), then invite volunteers to read aloud the following verses (as the verses are being read, turn the box around so the end you'll push outward will be the empty end). Read aloud Psalm 103:12, Romans 4:7, and Colossians 1:13, 14. Then ask:

- ✄ How has God provided for our forgiveness?
- ✄ What happens when we're forgiven through Jesus?
- ✄ Why do you suppose God removes our sins and remembers them no more?
- ✄ How can it give us a new beginning in life when we know we're forgiven?

Hold up the box and say: **What happens to our sins when we're forgiven?** Open the box and show kids how the "sins" inside have vanished. **They are removed and completely taken away! Isn't it wonderful that through Jesus' forgiveness, our sins are taken away?**

End by sharing a prayer thanking God for His power to forgive us through Jesus and for removing our sins completely when we ask for His mercy and forgiveness.

TERRIFIC TIP!

Try using this neat presentation with the secret box using a dime instead of the word card to accompany Jesus' parable of the lost coin. Begin by showing the coin, then placing it in the box. Secretly turn the box around to show how the coin became lost. When you reach the place in the parable where the coin is found, secretly turn the box around once more to reveal the dime!

Jesus Frees Us!

Romans 6:18, 22, 8:2

God's Power... Overcomes evil

Simple Supplies

- letter envelope
- scissors
- markers
- construcion paper

PREPARING THE TALK

Before class, cut a simple figure (with arms upraised) from construction paper. Use the illustration from page 63 as a guide. Make sure the figure is a couple of inches longer than the length of your envelope and is thinner in width. Use markers to add facial features, hair, and clothing. Set the figure aside for now.

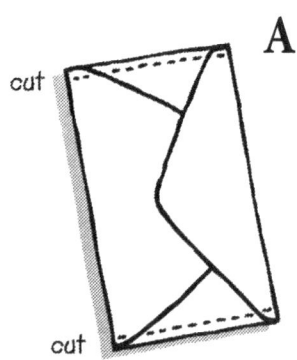

A

Prepare the envelope by first sealing it closed. Then cut off the end at each side (see illustration A). Then carefully poke the scissors through one layer of the envelope about an inch below one of the open ends. Cut across the end (only one layer) stopping about a half inch from either end (illustration B). Repeat for the opposite end.

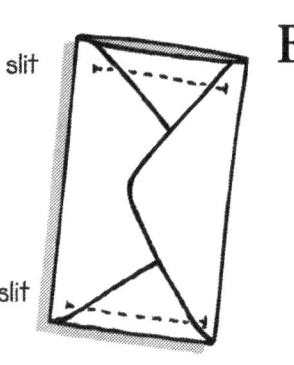

B

During the object talk, you'll be "threading" the figure through these two slits, so be sure to keep the slits facing away from the kids. Practice threading the figure smoothly through the back slits before your presentation. Use illustration D on the opposite page to see how the figure will look from the back and illustration C for how the figure will appear from the front.

During the object talk, it will appear to the kids as if you're cutting the figure in half...but really you'll be cutting *behind* the figure (illustration D). You may wish to practice the cutting several times (using several envelopes) to become familiar with how this slick trick works!

Have extra construction paper available for kids to make their own figures. You may wish to provide a figure to trace.

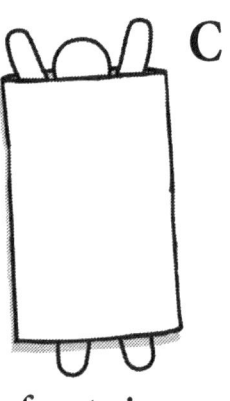

C

front view

PRESENTING THE POINT

Hold the envelope (slits away from kids) and the figure. Place the scissors beside you. Tell kids you want them to think about things that keep us trapped in our lives and how we can be set free from traps like evil, sin, temptation, and disobedience to God. Hold up the figure and say: **Let's pretend this represents us or represents people. When we love, follow, and obey God, we're free and feel joyous. But…** (thread the figure through the slits in the back of the envelope) **…there are many things that can trap us in life and take away that freedom and joy. Temptations to say or do the wrong things, sin, evil, and disobeying God all trap us in a place that's far from God. It's like being in an invisible jail that separates us from God and His love.** Ask:

- How does sin keep us trapped?
- Why do you think God desires us to be free of sin in our lives?
- In what ways are our lives affected when we disobey God?

back view

Say: **The Bible tells us that we've all sinned and fallen short of God's glory. And as we've all sinned and felt temptations, we all need to be set free. God has provided a way for us to be set free through His Son, Jesus! When we ask for Jesus' forgiveness and turn to follow Him in all we do, Jesus cuts the bonds that trap us…** (cut the envelope in back of the figure) **…and those bonds that threatened to tear us apart, drop off and we're whole and set free!** Pull out the uncut figure and hold it up.

Invite volunteers to read aloud Romans 6:18, 22, 8:2. Then say: **We're joyously free and made whole by God's power through Jesus! Where sin and evil caused us to be trapped and enslaved, Jesus set us free to live close to God forever. No wonder our paper figure looks so happy—and just imagine how joyous we are!**

Let kids make their own paper figures. Have them add their names to tell how glad they are that Jesus sets us free. If there's time and if you have enough envelopes, kids will enjoy learning how to do this cool trick. Challenge them to share the object talks at home with their families and friends as they remind others about the joyous freedom we have through God's power and Jesus!

Help = Love!

Galatians 5:13; 1 Thessalonians 5:14; Hebrews 6:10

God's Power...  Helps us day and night

Simple Supplies
- paper plates
- construction paper
- scissors
- markers
- glue sticks
- small pencils
- large paper clips

PREPARING THE TALK

Before class, collect the supplies including a paper plate, small pencil, and large paper clip for each person. Make a divided paper plate to show during the object talk. To make the plate, cut six construction paper wedges to fit around the inside circle on a paper plate. Use a variety of colors for the wedges if possible. (See the illustration on page 64.) Use markers to write the following chores, one per wedge:

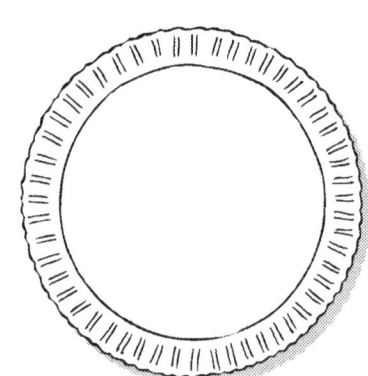

- Take out the trash.
- Wash the dishes..
- Fold the laundry.
- Clean out a closet.
- Sweep the garage.
- Mop the floor.

You'll be discussing everyday ways we can help others during this object talk. You'll need a plain paper plate, the plate you just prepared, a pencil, and a paper clip. Kids will be making Help-n-Serve Plates to take home along with pencils and paper clips to use as spinners (see the box below).

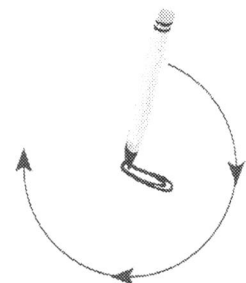

> Use a pencil and paper clip to make an instant spinner. Hold the pencil lead at one end of the paper clip, then spin the clip.

PRESENTING THE POINT

Place the plain paper plate beside you and hide the paper plate with the chores behind you along with the pencil and paper clip. Gather kids and hold up the plain paper plate. Ask:

✂ In what ways can a single paper plate be used?

✂ How can a simple paper plate be used to help someone?

✂ Do you think it's important to be willing to help others? Explain.

Say: **A paper plate might not seem very special or even useful in helping, but it can be used to serve foods, hold lunches that feed the hungry, or even carry a dinner to a sick friend. These may seem like small ways to help and serve, but every way we can offer help is a giant demonstration of love! God helps us in both large and small ways each day—and every way God helps us is a show of His love, too.** Ask:

✂ How does offering help pass along our love and kindness to others?

✂ In what ways does helping others tell God we love Him, too?

Say: **God's Word teaches us so much about helping and serving as God desires. Let's discover a bit about what we can learn by sharing a few verses.** Invite volunteers to read aloud Galatians 5;13b, 1 Thessalonians 5:14, and Hebrews 6:10. Then ask:

✂ What does God's Word tell us to do for others in need?

✂ What are ways you can offer help to others this week?

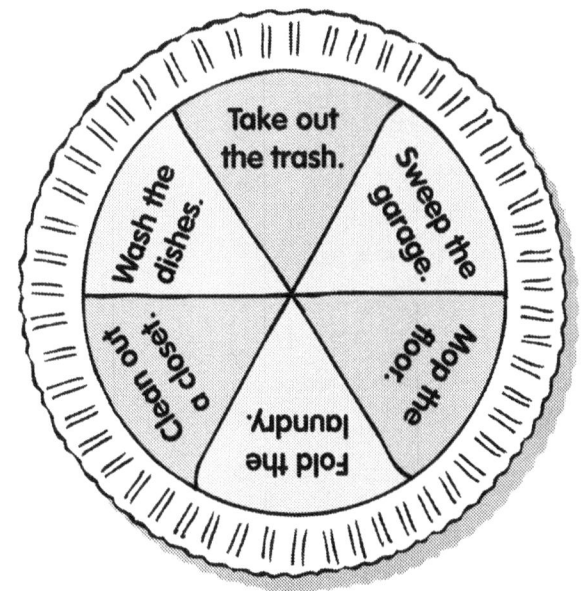

Encourage kids to tell they could do chores around the house, rake a neighbor's yard, or even send a cheery card to encourage a friend. Hold up the serving wheel and let kids take turn spinning the paper clip and reading the chore it lands on. Then hand out paper plates and let kids make their own Help-n-Serve Wheels to take home as they seek to help others as God helps us.

End with a prayer thanking God for His help in our own lives, then ask His power in finding ways to help and serve others during the week.

The Victory Is the Lord's
Psalm 24:8; Ephesians 6:13-18

God's Power... Gives us victory

Simple Supplies

- construction paper
- colored markers
- scissors
- a small square box
- craft glue
- fine-tipped, permanent black marker
- clear tape
- photocopies of the God's armor pieces from page 67

PREPARING THE TALK

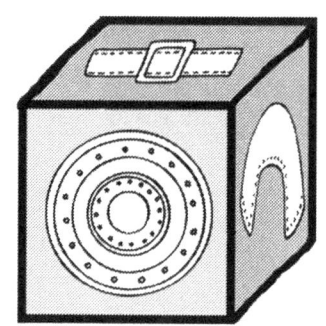

Before class, photocopy the God's armor pieces from page 67. Make a copy for each child plus an extra. Cover a small, square box with solid-colored construction paper or wrapping paper (paper grocery sacks will also work). Color the pattern pieces on the extra copy of God's armor, then cut out the pieces. Glue each piece of God's armor to a side of the box. During the object talk, kids will be rolling the cube and looking up, from Ephesians 6:14-17, the appropriate piece of God's armor. As a take-home reminder of our victory through God's power and armor, kids will draw themselves as "paper dolls" and attach the pieces of God's armor to the figures.

PRESENTING THE POINT

Place the game cube and a Bible beside you. Show kids the pictures on each side of the cube and ask if they know who wore these kinds of items and what they're used for. Lead kids to tell that these are pieces of equipment or armor that used to be worn in battle. Explain that in biblical days, there were many battles for land, for God, and between tribes of people. Then say: **There were many battles long ago waged for God and His chosen people. We have battles and wars today—and even in our own lives we battle things such as temptations, evil, and disobedience to God. We may not know exactly what the battle will be, but we do know who will win in the end and who has the power to win!** Invite volunteers to read aloud

Psalm 24:8 and 1 Corinthians 15:57. Then take turns rolling the cube and reading from Ephesians 6:13-18 to read the verses that correspond with the pieces of God's armor that were rolled on the cube. When all pieces have been rolled and verses read, say: **God provides us with special armor to battle evil, sin, and temptations. And when we take up God's armor and put it on each day, we know the victory will be ours! Let's make armored paper dolls to remind us of God's power and the victory He leads us to when we obey and follow Him, wearing God's full armor.**

Have kids draw outlines of themselves on construction paper. Then distribute copies of the armor patterns for kids to color, cut out and glue to their paper dolls. As you work, discuss how each piece of God's armor works to helps us win any battle we may face.

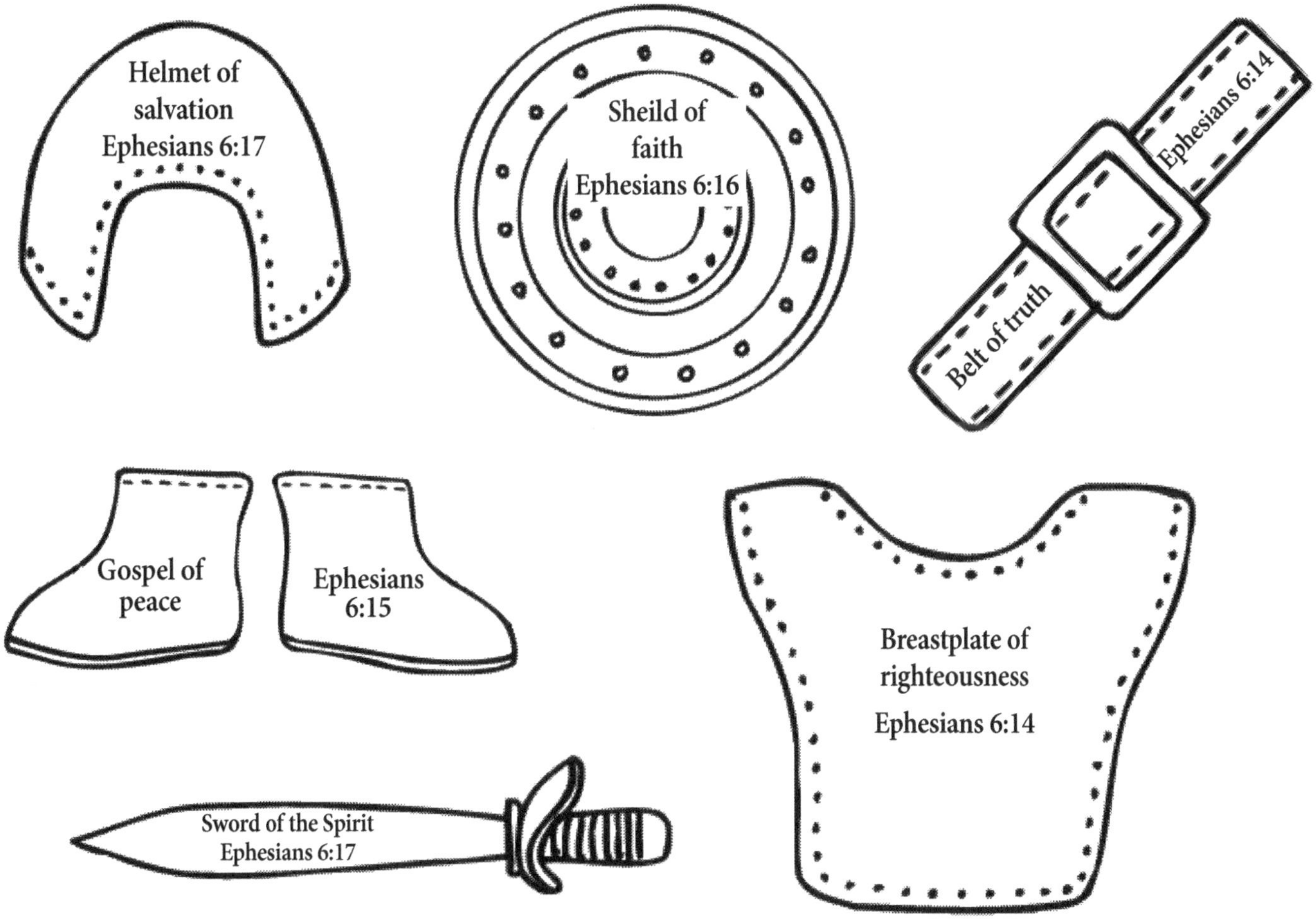

> **TERRIFIC TIP!**
> Use bits of aluminum foil for shiny touches.

Helmet of salvation
Ephesians 6:17

Sheild of faith
Ephesians 6:16

Belt of truth
Ephesians 6:14

Gospel of peace
Ephesians 6:15

Breastplate of righteousness
Ephesians 6:14

Sword of the Spirit
Ephesians 6:17

Permission to photocopy for church, school, or home use only. Taken from *20/20 Crafts & Object Talks That Teach About God's Power* © Susan Lingo, Susan Lingo Books, 2007.

The Road to Guidance

Psalms 25:5, 43:3

God's Power...

Directs and guides us

Simple Supplies

- copy paper
- scissors
- markers
- glitter glue pens
- old atlas pages or maps (to be cut into 8-inch squares)

PREPARING THE TALK

Before class, cut old maps or pages from an atlas into 8-inch squares, one for each child and one for yourself. You'll also need 8-inch squares of white copy paper to make paper cups from. Kids will also make cups from the map squares. Practice making a folded paper cup so you can direct kids as to how to fold the paper. To make a paper cup, follow these steps:

STEP 1: **Lay a square of paper on a table in a diamond shape (figure 1). Fold the bottom point upward to meet the top point (figure 2). Crease the paper well.**

STEP 2: **Fold the lower right corner over to the center of the opposite side (figures 3 & 4). Do the same for the lower left corner.**

STEP 3: **Fold the top points downward on each side (figure 5). Crease all folds well.**

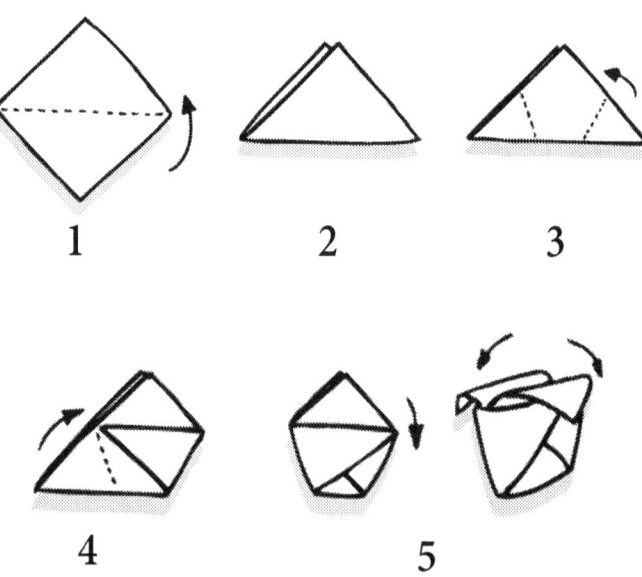

PRESENTING THE POINT

Gather kids in front of you as you hold the plain white paper cup you made before class. (Have the map squares and copy-paper squares beside you.) Ask kids if they know what you're holding, then tell them you read directions on how to make this cool cup to really drink from by reading a craft book. Ask:

- ✂ Why is it important to follow directions when making a craft project?
- ✂ What can happen to a craft if directions aren't followed correctly, completely, or carefully?
- ✂ How is this like following God's directions in our lives?
- ✂ How can we discover what God's directions for life are?

Say: **God's guidance and directions are found in His Word…the Bible. In the Bible, we find God's rules for living according to His plan and purpose. We discover all of God's truth, His power, and His ultimate wisdom.** Ask:

- ✂ Why is it important to obey God's directions?
- ✂ In what ways are God's directions like a road map for our lives?
- ✂ What can happen if we don't follow God's directions?

Read aloud Psalms 25:5 and 43:3. Discuss how we gain wisdom and understanding from God's Word; how that wisdom and guidance directs our choices, decisions, and faith. Then distribute the white paper squares and guide kids through folding paper cups. Remind them that following directions carefully is important! Then let kids make paper cups from the map squares. Point out that the Bible directs us as we travel through life much as a road map directs travelers on trips. Use markers and glitter glue pens to embellish the cups if desired.

If there's time, let kids copy Psalm 25:5 and 43:3 onto slips of colored paper to carry in their cups. Offer a prayer thanking God for His powerful directions for our lives through His Word.

TERRIFIC TIP!
Use large, bright squares of gift wrap to make celebration cups. Add slips of paper with praises for God's power written on them to present to friends or family members.

Rising to heaven
Psalm 141:2

God's Power... Hears our prayers

Simple Supplies

- incense cones (one per child plus one extra)
- metal jar lids (one per person)
- colored permanent markers
- tacky craft glue
- large plastic gems and jewels
- a small bag of sand
- matches
- photocopies of the card from page 71
- tape

PREPARING THE TALK

Before class, collect the items in the supply list. Be sure you have a clean, metal jar lid for each person and a cone of incense. Photocopy the verse cards from page 71, one card per person. Cut out the cards. You'll be lighting an incense cone, so make sure it is fine to do so in the room you're in—or step outside so children can smell the sweet incense and see it rising into the air. (Any scent will do, but if you find frankincense, myrrh, or sage it will work very well.)

You may wish to prepare a jar-lid incense holder to use as you burn the incense. Kids will be making these incense holders to carry home for their parents to light for dinner time or bedtime prayers.

To make the incense holder, color a clean, (large if possible) metal jar lid using colorful, permanent markers. Glue large, plastic gems and jewels around the sides of the lid to embellish it. (Add touches of glitter glue if desired.) Sprinkle a half-inch of sand in the bottom of the lid, then place a cone of incense in the center. The tip of the cone can be lighted by an adult. When the tip is glowing, allow the incense "smoke" to rise into the air. To extinguish the incense, simply rub the tip of the cone in the sand.

PRESENTING THE POINT

Set the incense lid and cone on a table or chair. Gather kids close by and explain that in Old Testament times, the priests would light a special herb or scent called "incense." Tell kids you're going to light a cone of incense for them to experience. Challenge kids to use their senses to describe what the incense is doing or what it is like. Tell kids they are not to talk—just use their senses.

Use a match to light the incense cone (keep the cone in the jar-lid holder). After the incense has been smouldering for several minutes, quietly kids to describe what they see and smell. Then ask:

✄ In what direction is the incense smoke rising?

✄ How does the incense smell?

✄ In what ways is sweet incense like sweet prayers to God?

✄ Does God always hear our prayers? Explain.

Say: **The Bible tells us that our prayers are sweet incense that rises to God. As incense is carried upward with sweet fragrance, our prayers are like sweet fragrances that rise to God. Why do you think our prayers are so sweet to God?** Encourage kids to share their thoughts and ideas. Then invite a volunteer to read aloud Psalm 141:2. Ask:

✄ Besides our prayers, what other things are like sweet incense rising to God?

✄ How is sharing our prayers with God a way of telling God we love Him?

Let kids make their own incense holders from the jar lids. Hand out the incense cones and verse cards for kids to take home with their holders.

- -

> • • • • • • • • • • • • • • •
> As sweet incense rises into the air,
> Our prayers rise to God who we know is there—
> To listen, to answer, to give us His love;
> Our incense-prayers rise to heaven above!
> —Psalm 141:2

> • • • • • • • • • • • • • • •
> As sweet incense rises into the air,
> Our prayers rise to God who we know is there—
> To listen, to answer, to give us His love;
> Our incense-prayers rise to heaven above!
> —Psalm 141:2

Permission to photocopy for church, school, or home use only. Taken from *20/20 Crafts & Object Talks That Teach About God's Power* © Susan Lingo, Susan Lingo Books, 2007.

Any Way, We're Okay!
Matthew 5:43-48

PREPARING THE TALK

Photocopy page 73. Use makers to add color to the page if desired. Practice folding and unfolding the paper according to the directions. The figure will begin in an upright position, then flip to an upside-down position, then repeat the steps to return the figure to an upright stance.

STEP 1: Fold page downward in half. Crease.

STEP 2: Fold right to left. Crease.

STEP 3: Swing the back over to the right.

STEP 4: Open the paper upward to reveal the upside down figure.

PRESENTING THE POINT

As you fold, chat about the kind of day we might have when things go awry and make us frustrated, upset, or even angry—and how we feel upside down! (Figure should be upside down at this point.) Remind kids that God loves them even on those days, and is ready to help us. Explain that as we trust God, our day becomes better until we're standing on top of the world again! (Figure should be right side up.)

God's Power...

Simple Supplies

- photocopy of page 73
- markers

Permission to photocopy for church, school, or home use only. Taken from *20/20 Crafts & Object Talks That Teach About God's Power* © Susan Lingo, Susan Lingo Books, 2007.

Healed Hearts
Psalm 34:18; Jeremiah 30:17

God's Power...
Heals us in many ways

Simple Supplies

- small paper or gift sack
- red construction paper
- tape or glue stick
- scissors
- photocopies of heart patterns from page 75 (on red construction paper)

PREPARING THE TALK

Before class, you'll need to prepare the secret-pocket sack. Cut a 6-inch construction paper square (as close a match to the sack as possible—you don't want kids to see the hidden pocket). Tape or glue the sides and bottom of the square to the *inside* of the paper sack to make a secret pocket. Cut out the red hearts you photocopied from the patterns on page 75 (or ones you've cut out yourself). Make sure the two hearts are the same size. Place one of the hearts in the hidden pocket. During the object talk, you'll tear the other heart and place the pieces in the bag. Then you'll carefully (and secretly) pull the whole heart from the hidden pocket to make it appear as if the heart has been amazingly made whole again. Practice this sleight of hand several times prior to your presentation. Cut out a large red cross and tape or glue it to the front of the sack.

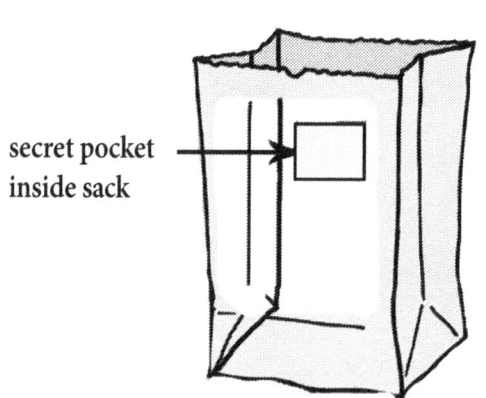

secret pocket inside sack

PRESENTING THE POINT

Place the sack with the hidden pocket in front of you being careful not to let the kids see the hidden pocket or the heart inside the pocket. Hold the other paper heart. Ask kids to tell about things that can hurt us such as mean words, selfish acts, or name calling. Then say: **There are so many times we may feel hurt, torn up, or sad. It's normal to feel this way at times—but it's not any fun. In fact, when we're feeling hurt or sad, it can stop**

us from serving God as He desires or from loving others with whole hearts as God desires. Tear the paper heart several times as you continue. **When we're feeling torn up, there's only one who can help us become whole again. Who do you suppose can heal our hearts, spirits, and feelings?** Lead kids to tell that only God can truly heal us.

When we give our hurt and broken hearts to God… (place the torn pieces in the bag and slyly remove the whole heart from the pocket) **…He makes our hearts whole and new again!** Hold up the whole paper heart and quickly set aside the paper sack. (Don't let kids see inside the sack!) Ask:

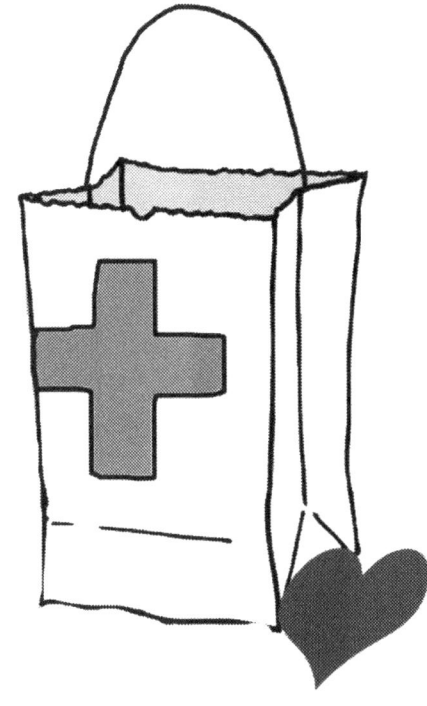

✂ How does God heal and help us?

✂ Why is it important to give our hurts to God for healing?

Read aloud Psalm 34:18 and Jeremiah 30:17 and briefly discuss how God may use other people to heal us—or allow us to help heal others with broken hearts. Discuss how God sent His only Son, Jesus, to heal, help, and forgive us. Then close by offering a prayer thanking God for His power to heal us and make our hearts like new.

Perfect Planning

Proverbs 23:18; Jeremiah 29:11

God's Power... Promises us a future

Simple Supplies

- white paper
- markers or pencils
- a paper sack or basket

PREPARING THE TALK

Before class, collect nine markers or pencils, a small basket or bag, and a sheet of white copy paper. This slick trick amazes kids—and is super-simple for you to present! During the object talk, you'll tear the sheet of paper into nine pieces: three across the top, center, and bottom. You'll hand a piece to each of nine kids—simply remember who you hand the center piece to. *Note that the center piece is the only piece with four rough-torn sides* (see the illustration on page 77—it is the shaded piece). It will appear as if you can tell the future when you identify what this child has written!

PRESENTING THE POINT

Place the markers or pencils and the small bag or basket on a table. Hold the sheet of copy paper and say: **Did you know that I can tell the future? I will choose some of you to write down a word or two about what you plan to do this weekend. Then I'll choose one of you—because I don't want to wear out my special powers—to tell what you've written about your future plans!**

Tear the paper and hand out each of the nine squares making sure you remember who you gave the four-torn sided piece to. Hand out the markers or pencils and have kids write a word or two about what they plan to do over the coming weekend. Then ask a volunteer to collect the nine pieces and place them in the bag or basket.

Look around the room and choose the child, to whom you gave the special square, to stand. Say: **I think I would like to tell *your* future** (name). **But first, I must try to find the words you chose to write from all these paper squares.**

Look around the room for effect, then remove the papers one-by-one. Hold each to your forehead (again, for effect) and shake your head slowly as you set each down and say "Not this one" or "Hmm …I don't think this is it." Continue until you remove the square with four torn sides. Then say, "I think this is it!" Read the paper aloud and ask the child to confirm if this is what he or she wrote.

After everyone has asked how you could tell the future, ask:

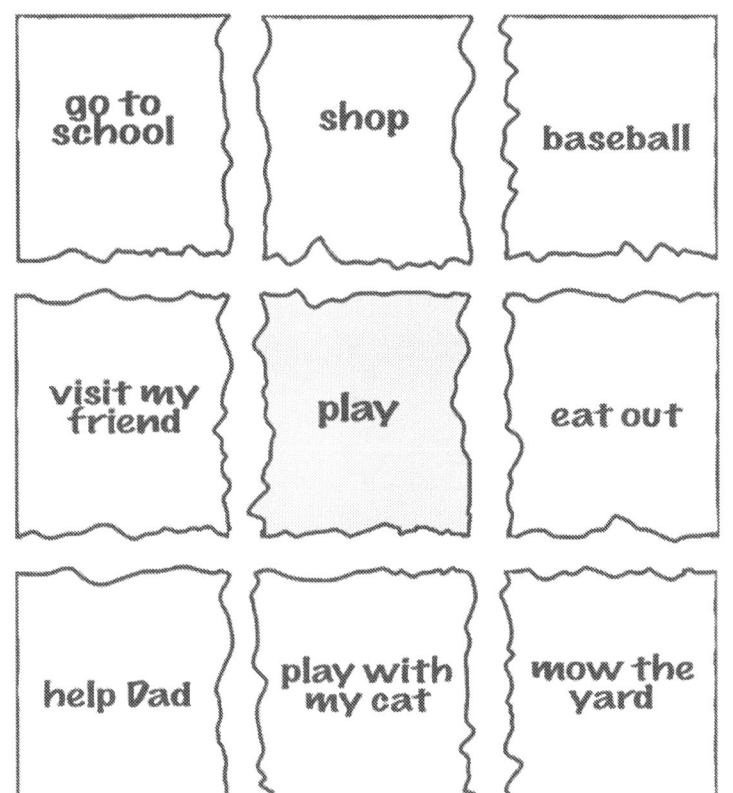

- ✂ Do you believe that I can truly tell the future or what is planned for tomorrow? Explain.

- ✂ Who is the only one wise and powerful enough to know the plans He has for you? to know the future?

- ✂ How does it help us trust God even more to know He is in control of the future and of His plans for us?

Explain to kids that telling what they'd do this weekend was only a fun trick-that you cannot tell the future. Remind them that only God has the power to know our futures—and that He has plans for each of us in that wonderful future.

Invite volunteers to read aloud Proverbs 23:18 and Jeremiah 29:11. Discuss what God's plans might include such as His plan for salvation through Jesus, His plan for us to live with Him in heaven, or even God's plan for the ultimate victory of good over evil and eternal life over eternal death. End with a prayer thanking God for His power to know the future and ask His direction in showing you the plans He has for all your tomorrows.

TERRIFIC TIP!

Have kids draw shapes instead of writing words. Or tear up several sheets of paper but only keep one center square. You'll be able to identify one child out of 25!

Not-So-Fishy Names
John 10:3

Simple Supplies

- scissors
- white card stock paper
- markers
- photocopies of the fish patterns from page 79 (on card stock, one fish per person)

PREPARING THE TALK

Before class, photocopy the fish patterns from page 77 on white card stock paper. Make one fish pattern per person, plus one for yourself. Cut out the fish patterns. Be sure you have one marker for each person, plus markers or crayons to use in coloring the fish patterns.

PRESENTING THE POINT

Seat kids in a circle on the floor. Distribute a paper fish and marker to each person. Tell kids to flip their fish over and write the name of a particular fish, such as a bass, on the back. When everyone has written a name, direct kids to flip the fish over and write their own names on the front of the fish. After all the names have been written, read the names of the fish (on the backs) one by one. If anyone has the same fish name, lay those fish in the center of the circle. Continue until all the fish names have been read. Then ask:

✄ **Are these the only names for fish? Explain.**

✄ **Could we possibly know all the names for all types of fish? Why not?**

✄ **How is this like trying to learn all the names of the people in the world?**

Retrieve the fish, then have kids read their names on the fronts of the fish. If anyone has the same name, lay those fish in the center of the circle. Continue until all the kids' names have been read. Then ask:

✄ **Does anyone know every person's name? Explain.**

✂ How does God know everyone's name?

Say: **It would be impossible for any of us to know everyone's name in the world! But God's power allows Him to know everyone's name—and even what each person is like on the inside. He knows each of our dreams and thoughts; He knows our feelings and where we live; and God even knows what is in our deepest hearts! No one knows us as God knows us.** Ask:

✂ How does it affect your faith and trust to know that God knows you by name and knows your every thought?

Invite volunteers to read aloud John 10:3 and write the verse on the fronts of their fish. Color the fish. Encourage kids to hang their fish in their rooms as colorful reminders of how God calls them by name and knows them by heart.

Permission to photocopy for church, school, or home use only. Taken from *20/20 Crafts & Object Talks That Teach About God's Power* © Susan Lingo, Susan Lingo Books, 2007.

The Clean Machine
2 Timothy 2:20, 21

Simple Supplies

- a medium sized jar & lid
- rocks
- small pebbles
- sand or aquarium gravel
- water
- a cup of potting soil
- a plastic spoon

PREPARING THE TALK

Before class, prepare a small aquifer by placing rocks at the bottom of a jar. Place a layer of sand over the rocks and small pebbles or aquarium gravel on top of that. Fill the jar with water. During this object talk, you'll spoon a small amount of potting soil into the water and watch as it filters downward through the layers in the jar. If you'd like kids to make their own aquifer jars, provide small jars and lids, rocks, pebbles, and sand.

PRESENTING THE POINT

Place the cup of potting soil, plastic spoon, and cleansing jar on the table in front of the kids. Ask if they know what an "aquifer" is for. Then explain that an aquifer is a layer of rocks, pebbles, and sand that water runs through. As the water runs through the layers, it is cleansed and made purer to drink. Tell kids that God placed a natural aquifer under the ground so that water that seeps through the aquifer is made cleaner, nicer, and more pure.

Discuss what kinds of things can make us unclean in God's eyes. Suggestions might include lies, cheating, hurting others, saying bad words, and disobeying God. Open the jar lid and scoop potting soil onto the plastic spoon. Say: **Let's pretend like this soil represents the unclean things we put into our lives.** Place the spoonful of potting soil into the water and let kids watch as the soil sinks its way down through the pebbles, the sand, and the larger rocks to settle at the bottom. As the soil is settling, say: **The aquifer cleanses the soil from the water so that the water is cleaner and made pure again.** Ask:

- ✂ How is this like the ways God cleanses us?
- ✂ In what ways does God provide for us to be cleansed and made pure?
- ✂ How does Jesus help us become clean and like new?

Read aloud 2 Timothy 2:20, 21. Then say: **God's power provides for us to be cleansed so we can approach Him and be close to Him. God desires us to be clean, pure, and made like new—and He sent Jesus as our wonderful "aquifer" for sin, evil, and temptation! Through Jesus, we're made new and clean—and are forgiven of the things that made us so unclean. As you drink water today, remember how God cleanses us through His love and power!**

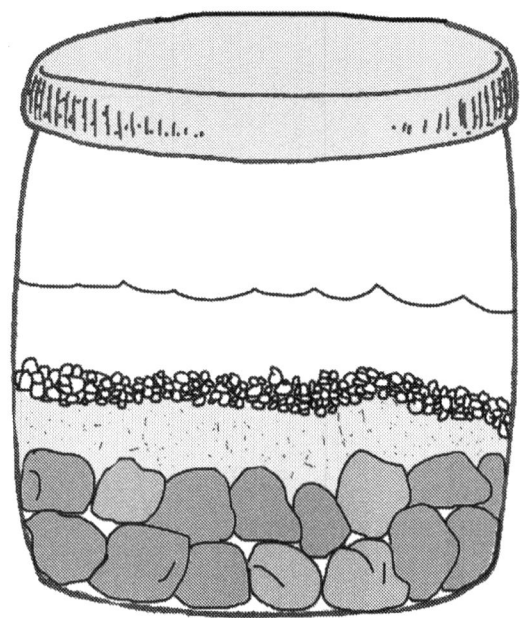

TERRIFIC TIP!

If there's time, let kids make their own small aquifers. Place a verse card of 2 Timothy 2:20, 21 on the top of the jar lid.

For Another Kind of Clean…

Try cleansing pennies or other coins using salt and lemon juice. Let kids scrub away with old toothbrushes by dipping the coins in lemon juice, then scrubbing them with salt. A final rinse in clean water should make your coins sparkle and shine!

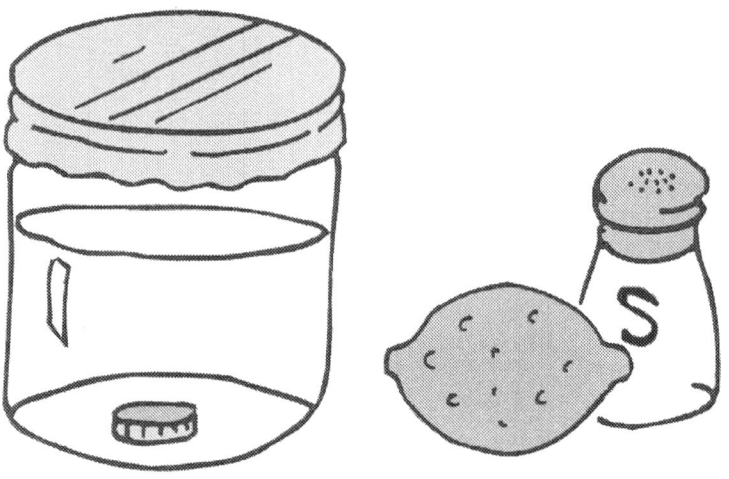

Guardian Angels
Psalm 91:9-16

God's Power... Protects us

Simple Supplies

- plastic spoons
- scissors
- markers & crayons
- fine-tipped, permanent black markers
- white card stock paper
- photocopies of the angel robe and wings from page 83 (on card stock, one set per person)
- metallic chenille wires (optional)

PREPARING THE TALK

Before class, photocopy the angel robe and wing patterns on white card stock paper, one set of patterns for each person plus one for yourself. Be sure you have a plastic spoon for everyone.

Use a plastic spoon to assemble an angel before class. (Use a fine-tipped, permanent black marker for facial features.) Kids will be making their own guardian angels to take home as reminders of God's protective powers. If you wish, provide paper doilies, scraps of fabric or ribbon, metallic chenille wires, and glitter glue to embellish the angels.

PRESENTING THE POINT

Hold up the angel you made earlier and ask kids to tell what they know about God's angels. Suggestions might include that angels are God's messengers, angels are sent by God to watch over us, and angels are sent to help us. Say: **God's angels are also our special protectors! God's power protects us and one way is by His angels. We read about the way angels protected many of God's people in the Bible including Paul and Peter. And**

Psalm 91 tells us all about God's protective power and the power He gives to angels. Invite volunteers to read aloud Psalm 91:9-16, then ask:

- ✄ How does God protect us every moment of the day and night?
- ✄ What do angels do for us through God's power?
- ✄ How does it feel to know that God and His angels are watching over and protecting you?

Remind kids that angels have the power to protect us because God directs them to do so—and because God loves us so greatly. Invite kids to make their own "guardian angels." End by sharing a prayer thanking God for His powerful love and for covering us with His angels.

- -

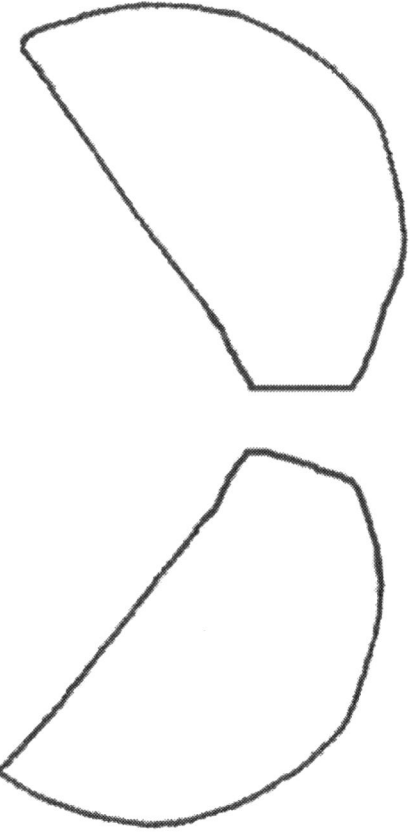

Permission to photocopy for church, school, or home use only. Taken from *20/20 Crafts & Object Talks That Teach About God's Power* © Susan Lingo, Susan Lingo Books, 2007.

Stop the Pop!
Matthew 6:25-34

God's Power...
Takes care of the details

Simple Supplies

- 3 medium sized balloons (plus several extra for practicing)
- 2 straight pins
- clear tape

PREPARING THE TALK

Before class, collect the simple materials. Be sure you have extra balloons to practice with before the object talk time. (You'll need three inflated balloons for the actual talk.) Inflate a balloon and place a small piece of clear tape on the side. (You will keep this piece of tape hidden from the kids during the object talk.) Carefully poke the pin into the balloon in the *center* of the tape. The balloon should not pop if you're in the center of the tape. Leave the pin in place during the talk or the balloon will pop. You will be inviting a volunteer to poke a pin in a balloon as you just did—but you'll "forget" to tell him about the tape and, of course, the balloon will pop. After learning about the tape, the volunteer will try again with a new balloon. (Let the volunteer us the second pin as you'll be leaving the first pin in your balloon.)

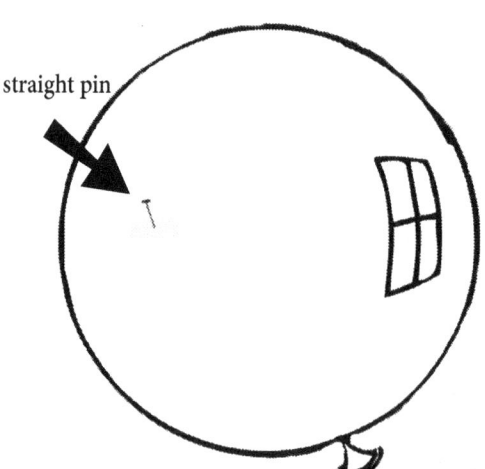

straight pin

PRESENTING THE POINT

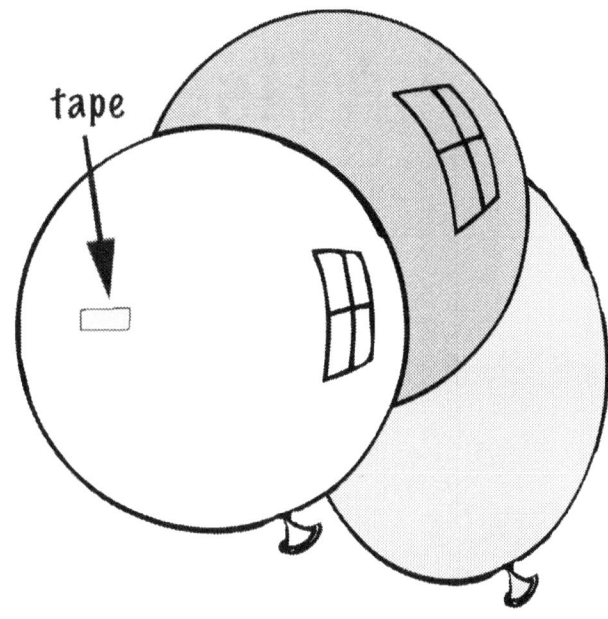

Hold the straight pin and the balloon with the clear tape (don't let kids see the tape on the balloon). Set the other two inflated balloons on a table. Keep the roll of tape hidden or in your pocket. Say: **I have a great thing to show you. I just learned how to do this cool trick and I want to share it with you! What happens when you stick a sharp pin in a balloon?** Let kids tell you that it pops. Then say: **It usually pops, but I know how to stop a pop! Watch this…** . Carefully stick the balloon into the center of the tape to prevent it from popping (don't tell the kids about the tape yet and leave the pin in place). **Wow! I stopped the pop! Who would like to try this cool trick?**

Choose a volunteer to come to the table and say: **I'll give you directions to follow, okay? First choose a balloon.** Pause for the volunteer to choose a balloon. Then continue: **Now you need a straight pin. Here …you can borrow this one.** Give the second straight pin to the child. Then say: **Now carefully poke the pin into the balloon like I did and you can stop the pop.** When the balloon pops, say: **Oh my! I wonder what went wrong…** (pause for effect, then continue) **Oh, I know! I left out a very important detail! You need tape!**

Show the volunteer how to place the tape on the balloon, then carefully poke the pin through the center of the tape. When the balloon doesn't pop, say: **I guess that one detail was the key! Why are details so important to anything and everything?** Encourage kids to share their ideas, then discuss how God supplies even the smallest details in all He does and all He teaches us. Ask:

- **What might happen if God didn't supply all the details of His Word or the world?**

- **Could we understand God's Word if He left out important details? Explain.**

- **If God is taking care of the details, is there any reason for us to worry? Why not?**

Read aloud Matthew 6:25-24 and discuss how God cares for the details so we don't have to worry about them. Close by letting kids inflate balloons and decorating them with permanent markers. Have them write Matthew 6:34 on their balloons. Challenge kids to put tape on their balloons at home and poke pins through the center of the tape as they remind their families how God supplies amazing details in our lives.

Wisecream Cones

Proverbs 2:6, 3:13, 8:11

God's Power... Gives us wisdom

Simple Supplies

- ice cream cones
- fiberfill
- craft glue
- small red beads
- satin ribbon
- scissors
- copies of the verse cards from page 87

PREPARING THE TALK

Before class, collect two empty ice cream cones (a cup style and a pointed cone). If you wish to have kids make their own ice cream cone projects, be sure you have a cone for each person. Make an "ice cream cone" to show kids by gluing fiberfill into the top of a cone. Glue a red bead to the top as a pretend cherry and add a loop for hanging on the side of the cone using ribbon. (You can omit the craft idea and simply present the object talk using empty cone shells.)

PRESENTING THE POINT

Hold up the two, empty ice cream cones. Ask kids what they are and if they are missing anything. Say: **These ice cream cones are just shells—they're missing the best part which is the sweet, goodness of ice cream. Without the sweetness, these cones are pretty boring and not really usable as they're meant to be.** Ask:

- How is an empty ice cream cone like people without God's wisdom inside their hearts?
- How can filling our lives with God's wisdom make us usable for God?

Say: **God's wisdom comes from His Word, which the Bible tells us is sweet!** Read aloud Proverbs 2:6, 3:13 and 8:11. Then discuss why God's Word is sweetness in our lives and how it helps us become all God desires us to be. Ask:

✂ How are we as easy-to-crush as an empty cone when we're not filled with God's wisdom?

✂ What kinds of things does God's wisdom teach us?

✂ How can we fill our lives with God's wisdom?

Distribute empty ice cream cones to the kids. Show them how to glue fiberfill into the cones as pretend ice cream. Sprinkle glitter on top of the pretend ice cream if desired. Have kids glue small, red beads to the tops of their cones as cherries. Then help kids use a hot glue gun to attach lengths of satin cord to the sides of the cones to make hanging loops. Finally, hot glue a verse card to the sides of the cones (or let kids write Proverbs 2:6 using fine-tipped, permanent markers directly on their cones).

Challenge kids to hang their special treats up at home to remind them that without filling our lives with God's wisdom, we're empty shells that can be cracked as easily as empty ice cream cones!

- -

For the LORD gives wisdom… —Proverbs 2:6	For the LORD gives wisdom… —Proverbs 2:6
For the LORD gives wisdom… —Proverbs 2:6	For the LORD gives wisdom… —Proverbs 2:6

Choice Obedience
Psalm 119:57, 66

God's Power...  **Helps us obey Him**

Simple Supplies
- sheets of construction paper
- scissors
- tape
- markers
- glitter glue (optional)

PREPARING THE TALK

Before class, weave a simple paper place mat by first cutting six or seven slits through the width of a sheet of construction paper. (Don't cut through the ends—come to within 2-inches of each end of the paper as in illustration A.) Cut 2-inch wide strips of construction paper (in various colors) and weave in and out, up and down across the paper (illustration B). Continue weaving strips across the page until the slits have been filled. Trim the ends (tape them if desired). If you'd like kids to make their own woven reminders of obeying God, provide paper strips and sheets of construction paper.

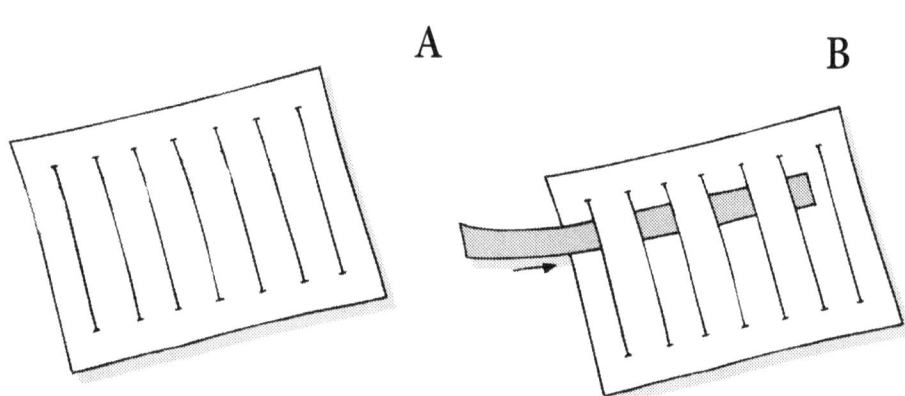

PRESENTING THE POINT

Hold the woven paper place mat in one hand and the fabric hankie in the other. Say: **I have a woven place mat, a fabric hankie, and myself here. What do all three of us have in common? Think hard!** Encourage kids to tell their ideas, which might include you're all made to be used or be productive and you're all created by someone. Lead kids to tell that the hankie, the place mat, and people are all woven in some way.

Say: **The hankie is woven up and down, in and out using fabric. The paper place mat is woven up and down, in and out using paper strips. And people are made up of woven choices and decisions that affect their lives. If we obey God when we have choices to make, we become woven tightly to Him. But if we make disobedient choices, it's like we dropped a stitch or made a bad error in our weaving—and we become filled with holes that make us liable to fall apart!** Ask:

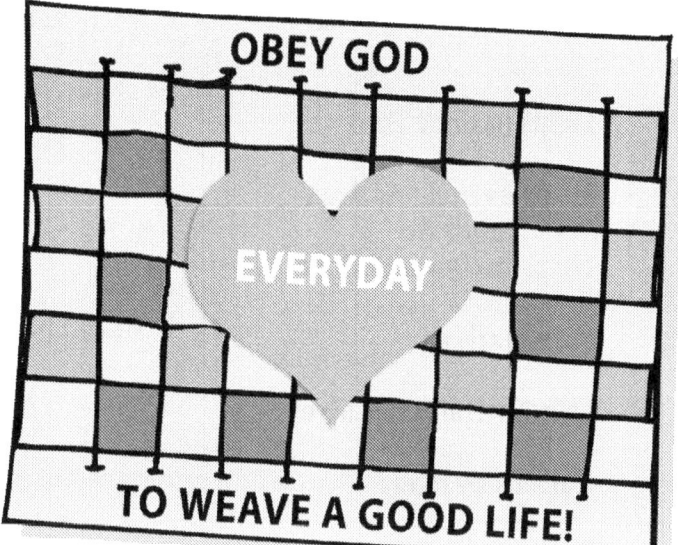

- Why is it important to make choices that are obedient to God?
- How does obedience draw us closer to God?
- In what ways does disobedience push us farther from God?
- How do our choices—both good and bad—weave throughout our whole lives and throughout our faith lives as well?

Say: **Just as this paper place mat was made of strips that were woven tightly over and under, up and down, and in and out, our lives are woven with choices that bring us into God's presence or push us out of God's presence. We become a woven tapestry, like a cloth, throughout our lives. And we want to obey God as we weave tightly with Him!**

If there's time, invite kids to make their own woven place mats. Encourage them to weave the strips tightly together as you remind them how obedient choices weave us more tightly to God. When the place mats are finished, have kids use markers to write words of wisdom about obeying God or to add Psalm 119:57—"I have promised to obey your words"—on their place mats. Laminate the mats or cover them in clear self-adhesive paper for durability.

Activities & Themes Index

God's Power …	Craft Activity	Object Talk
Helps us obey Him	page 8	page 88
Heals us in many ways	page 10	page 74
Helps us day and night	page 12	page 64
Surrounds us	page 14	page 54
Demonstrates His love	page 16	page 58
Calls us by name	page 18	page 78
Protects us	page 20	page 82
Accepts us	page 22	page 72
Helps us resist evil	page 24	page 52
Teaches us	page 26	page 56
Directs and guides us	page 28	page 68
Cleanses us	page 30	page 80
Hears our prayers	page 32	page 70
Takes care of the details	page 34	page 84
Promises us a future	page 36	page 76
Forgives us	page 38	page 60
Answers our prayers	page 40	page 50
Gives us victory	page 42	page 66
Gives us wisdom	page 44	page 86
Overcomes evil	page 46	page 62

NEW from Susan Lingo Books!

Making Scripture Memorable is one easy-to-use resource that effectively teaches a variety of Scripture verses in exciting, age-appropriate ways so an entire class, church, or family can stay on the "same page" growing and going for God! Simple-to-use activities and clever ideas for each verse are presented every week for three age levels including preschool/kindergarten, elementary, and youth/adult. Unique, fun for all ages, and powerfully effective, *Making Scripture Memorable* puts God's Word in everyone's hearts and minds at the same time!

ISBN 978-0-9760696-1-4

Calling all preschool leaders: Looking for ways to save your sanity? Just fill four ordinary boxes with simple, everyday items—then use the new ideas in this great resource to transform those boxes into …
- Creative, no-mess crafts
- Super stories and songs
- Lively games and rhymes
- Quiet-time learning centers
- Sanity-saving secrets

These ideas and activities are so flexible, you can pull out a winner on a moment's notice! *Sanity Savers* is sure to become your best friend and classroom helper in no time!

ISBN 978-0-9760696-2-1

Available from www.susanlingobooks.com or www.amazon.com!

Serving others is as easy as 1-2-3 with clever crafts that double as service projects! Each Bible-centered project allows kids to share their creative gifts and talents with others in the church, community, or with their families and friends. Every *Make-n-Serve* activity engages even hard-to-motivate kids with projects that are too big—and too much fun—to ignore. All activities come complete with quick-n-easy instructions so you'll have kids creating and serving in no time at all. Perfect for offering kids Bible-based learning fun in a *BIG* way!

ISBN 978-0-9760696-0-7

Get ready for the first powerful resource to teach how memory works and how kids (and even adults) can effectively learn to memorize God's Word! Activity sections for 3- to 6-year-olds and 7- to 12-year-olds, plus a special section on basic Bible skills. Interactive games, crafts, relay races, rhythm activities, songs, and much more provide countless ways to share God's Word as you share fun and faith!

ISBN 978-0-9760696-5-2

Looking for more great resources? You've come to the right place!

Object Talks

PRODUCT #	PRODUCT TITLE	PRICE PER ITEM	QUANTITY	TOTAL
1154-2	101 Simple Service Projects	$13.99		
1370-7	Quick Quiz Talk Starters	$13.99		
2022-4	Show Me! Devotions	$12.99		
7440-7	Show Me More! Object Talks	$12.99		
7441-7	20/20 Crafts & Object Talks	$12.99		
1417-7	Collect-n-Do Object Talks	$13.99		
1237-9	A to Z Object Talks (New Testament)	$5.99		
1236-0	A to Z Object Talks (Old Testament)	$5.99		
1838-X	Bible Message Make-n-Takes	$12.99		
1429-0	Preschool Bible Message Make-n-Takes	$12.99		
1184-4	Edible Object Talks (Jesus)	$5.99		
1183-6	Edible Object Talks (Values)	$5.99		

Crafts & Games

PRODUCT #	PRODUCT TITLE	PRICE PER ITEM	QUANTITY	TOTAL
7449-7	Make-n-Serve Crafts & Service Projects	$10.99		
7441-7	20/20 Crafts & Object Talks	$12.99		
5695-7	Instant Games for Children's Ministry	$13.99		
1199-2	Collect-n-Play Games	$13.99		
1198-4	Collect-n-Make Crafts	$13.99		
1838-X	Bible Message Make-n-Takes	$12.99		

Bibles & Bible Storytelling

PRODUCT #	PRODUCT TITLE	PRICE PER ITEM	QUANTITY	TOTAL
7450-7	Kids-Tell-Em Bible Stories	$11.99		
0406-6	My Good Night Bible	$14.99		
1228-X	My Little Good Night Bible	$9.99		
1174-7	My Good Night StoryBook	$14.99		
1229-8	My Little Good Night StoryBook	$9.99		
1365-0	My Good Night Prayers	$14.99		
1522-X	Christmas With Night Light	$10.99		
1362-0	Bedtime for Night Light (coloring book)	$3.99		
1418-5	Collect-n-Tell Bible Stories	$13.99		

POWER BUILDERS (2-Year Curriculum)

PRODUCT #	PRODUCT TITLE	PRICE PER ITEM	QUANTITY	TOTAL
7550-7	Disciple Makers	$12.99		
7554-7	Faith Finders	$12.99		
7552-7	Servant Leaders	$12.99		
7556-7	Value Seekers	$12.99		
7551-7	Hope Finders	$12.99		
7555-7	Joy Builders	$12.99		
7557-7	Power Boosters	$12.99		
7553-7	Peace Makers	$12.99		

Teacher Ideas & Learning Centers

PRODUCT #	PRODUCT TITLE	PRICE PER ITEM	QUANTITY	TOTAL
5525-X	Sanity Savers for Preschool Teachers	$12.99		
7444-7	Instant Learning Fun-Folders OT (CD)	$9.99		
7445-7	Instant Learning Fun-Folders NT (CD)	$9.99		
1332-4	200+ Activities for Children's Ministry	$12.99		
7442-7	Bulletin Boards That Teach	$13.99		
7443-7	Simple Celebrations for Children's Ministry	$12.99		

Bible Memory, Bible Skills, & Worship Activities

PRODUCT #	PRODUCT TITLE	PRICE PER ITEM	QUANTITY	TOTAL
7446-7	Scripture Memory Makers	$12.99		
7445-7	Making Scripture Memorable	$12.99		
7448-7	Basic Bible Skills	$13.99		
7447-7	Worship Wow!	$12.99		

Best Buy!

You can order two easy ways:

1. Directly from *Susan Lingo Books* through check or money order, or

2. from Amazon.com.

Send your check or money order (including shipping and handling) along with your order to:

Susan Lingo Books
3310 N. Logan Ave.
Loveland, CO 80538

Handling ($1.50 per order)	$1.50

Shipping:
Standard Book Rate:
  1-3 books—$10.50
  4+ books—$12.00 + $1.50 each
    additional book
Priority USPS:
  1 book—$16.00
  2+ books—$18.00 + $2.00 each
    additional book	

Subtotal of S/H	
Subtotal of books ordered	
TOTAL	

www.susanlingobooks.com